Rajasthan

Rajasthan

Text by
SEVANTI NINAN

Photographs by
SONDEEP SHANKAR

ROLI BOOKS INTERNATIONAL
New Delhi · Allahabad · Madras

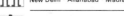

FEP INTERNATIONAL PRIVATE LIMITED
Accra · Hong Kong · Karachi · Kingston · Kuwait · Lagos · London · Manila · Maseru
Mbabane · Nairobi · New Delhi · Petaling Jaya · Port-of-Spain · Singapore · Sydney

Acknowledgments

The publishers wish to thank the following for their valuable assistance: Professor Rajat K. Ray of Presidency College, Calcutta; Archaeological Survey of India; and Rajasthan Information Centre, New Delhi.

First published 1980 by
Roli Books International
4378/4 Ansari Road, Daryaganj
New Delhi

Designed by
Promodini Varma

Printed and bound by
FEP International Private Limited, Jurong, Singapore

Contents

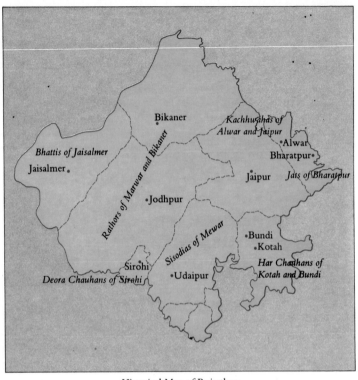

Historical Map of Rajasthan

Introduction

RAJASTHAN — THE ABODE OF PRINCES. THE NAME was given after it was all over: the pomp and pageantry of the Rajput court with its marble-inlaid palaces, pampered harems, and royal pastimes of poetry and chase. The occasion for valour and bloodshed was also past by the time the once fiercely independent princely state of Rajputana (as the area was formerly called) came to accede to the Indian Union in 1947. But in naming the newly formed state Rajasthan, the Indian Government seemed to be making a bow, as it were, to a proud, romantic tradition.

Remnants of the princely tradition still survive. The land is studded with fortresses and palaces, and cenotaphs erected in memory of members of Rajput royalty. The rest can be found in museums: the fabulous jewellery and costumes, the paintings done under royal patronage, and rare items from the collection of individual maharajas.

The notion of princely descent is also incorporated in the name of the race that came to establish itself in these parts. The word Rajput is a simplification of *raj-putra*, the son of a prince. Rajputs have been the dominant race in Rajasthan since about the eleventh century AD and claim not only princely but also divine descent.

Various Rajput clans trace their lineage back to figures in Hindu mythology. Places like Bairath near Alwar, Pushkar, and Jaisalmer are believed to have been the locale of episodes from the great Hindu epics, the *Ramayana* and the *Mahabharata*, and from the ancient Hindu texts, the Puranas.

Royalty and divinity apart, much of Rajasthan's vitality comes from its ordinary people. They provide the vivid colour — the rustic's turban is always yellow, orange, red or bright pink against the grey and brown of rock and desert. And it is their chiselling,

7

weaving, enamelling and tie-and-dyeing that fills elegant shops with handicrafts coveted the world over.

Life has not changed much in Rajasthan's 33,000 villages since the days of the princes. The Rajasthanis still marry off their children very early, flock en masse to weddings, festivals and fairs and migrate in search of work in the dry months when they cannot farm. Their staple food is *rotis* made of maize or barley flour, and *rabri*, a savoury porridge made of maize kernels cooked in buttermilk.

Folk music and dance, now a big draw in the cities, is still nurtured in these villages, where fledgling minstrels draw their first crowds.

Rajasthan has so much to offer. When you are through with its forts, palaces, dances, music and crafts, the land itself remains. It has miles of daunting desert, with dunes perfect down to the last ripple, hills that change colour with the season, marshes that come alive with birds, and sprawling sanctuaries where blackbuck, tigers and chinkara roam. There is always almost too much to see and do.

Below: A glimpse of rugged Chittor Fort.

Above left: An old woman savours a puff at the hookah.
Above right: An old villager, in his bespattered clothes, celebrating Holi.
Bottom: Young men listening to a transistor in a village near Ajmer.

Above: A youthful bridegroom on his way to his wedding. In rural Rajasthan, child marriages are still widely prevalent.
Above right: A Gujar boy playing on a local instrument called the *algoocha*.
Right: A Beharupia, a Rajasthan tribe of wandering performers.

Opposite: The princely order may have vanished but rustic traditions still hark back to the days of the Maharajas. A bridegroom sports the portrait of an Udaipur Maharaja in a brooch in his turban.

Above left: Bangle seller in Jodhpur.
Above right: A brass merchant in Udaipur's Sarafa Bazaar.
Left: A *dhelak* (drum) maker and his family from Kotah, in eastern Rajasthan.

History

To the uninitiated, Rajasthan's early history will seem a bewildering melange of clan and family names thrown up by successive waves of migrations which trace their mythological origins as far back as the sun and the moon. But you have to plough through this with a little forbearance, because the positioning of various clans is vital to an understanding of the events which shaped Rajasthan's history.

To begin at the beginning, Rajasthan's first known inhabitants were not Rajputs but the aboriginal tribes who have always lived in its hills. After the fourth century BC, the Mauryans occupied the area around Jaipur and Ajmer. They were the first Aryan dynasty to consolidate an empire in India. Even as court chronicles and temple inscriptions are the sources for medieval Rajasthani history, bits of neo-black polished pottery excavated near Jaipur and Ajmer are the clue to Mauryan settlements here.

Subsequent settlements followed in the early years of the Christian era. By the seventh century AD, a new set of warrior clans, who later came to be known as the Rajputs, had settled in Rajasthan. The hills, forests, and deserts of this area served as a natural refuge for the martial tribes of the surrounding regions, when pressed by foreign invaders. Geography shaped history: the Rajputs came here for refuge from Gujarat, the Punjab and the Gangetic valley, and gradually occupied all the great expanse of this area.

Who were the Rajputs? Supposed to be Aryan in origin, they claimed descent from the old solar, lunar and fire-born families of the Kshatriyas, a martial caste, next in the social heirarchy to the Brahmins. However, Colonel James Tod, the nineteenth century British political agent and Resident in Rajasthan, who first collected their annals in his monumental work, *Annals and Antiquities of*

Rajasthan, was sceptical of these mythological origins. He advanced the theory that many of these tribes, especially the fire-born clans, were Scythic barbarians from Central Asia who had been converted to Hinduism through the fire purification ceremony. But a noted Indian historian, Gaurishankar Ojha, has contested this theory and claims that there is nothing unlikely in Rajput clans being descended from the older Kshatriya tribes of ancient India.

The Rajputs have their own divisions. Originally they were supposed to have been divided into two principal and coordinate branches, styled "Suryavanshi" or solar race, and "Chandravanshi" or lunar race. Four "Agnicula" or fire-born races were added to these. According to mythology, the subsequent subdivisions of these races gave rise to thirty-six Rajput clans. Each clan had its own sub-races and families.

The important solar descendants who formed kingdoms in Rajasthan were the Guhilots or Sisodias of Mewar (Chittor and Udaipur), the Rathors of Marwar (Jodhpur) and the Kachhwahas of Amber and Jaipur. The Bhattis of Jaisalmer claimed to be lunar descendants. And the Chauhans of Delhi and Ajmer and their branches at Sirohi in the south-west and Bundi in the south-east traced their origin to the four mounted warriors who, according to legend, emerged from the sacrificial fire at Mount Abu.

Between the seventh century and the beginning of the eleventh century, several Rajput dynasties arose. The Guhilots, who later came to be called the Sisodias, migrated from Gujarat and occupied south-eastern Mewar. Their earliest inscription in Rajputana is dated AD 646.

Next came the Parihars who occupied Marwar until the Rathors seized power from them in the fourteenth century. The Parihars were followed in the eighth century by the Chauhans and Bhattis who settled near Ajmer and Jaisalmer respectively. Lastly, in the tenth century, two less important tribes began to spread their influence in the south-west. Of these early clans only the Sisodias, Bhattis, and Chauhans continued to rule over the next seven to eight hundred years, with the first two remaining in their original settlements and the Chauhans dispersing south-east to Bundi and Kotah, and south-west to Sirohi.

The other later Rajput clans who established themselves in

Rajputana and continued to rule till the nineteenth century were the Kachhwahas, who came to Jaipur from Gwalior early in the twelfth century, and the Rathors from Kanauj, who settled in Marwar at the beginning of the thirteenth century.

The second major Muslim invasion of India occurred in the eleventh century. The invaders, who were from Ghazni, found Rajput dynasties firmly ensconced in all the chief cities of northern India. Mahmud of Ghazni left a settlement in the Punjab but did not attempt to found a Muslim empire in India. His army once nearly perished of thirst in the desert of Rajputana, being misled by a false guide whom the prince of Jaisalmer had inserted in his camp to take revenge on the invader.

But the clans were weakened by a feud between the Rathors of Kanauj and the Chauhans of Delhi and Ajmer. The hostility was aggravated by a romance which has been celebrated since in ballad and verse.

Prithviraj Chauhan, the ruler of Delhi and Ajmer, was a gallant, noble and somewhat imprudent prince. Legends about him had stirred the imagination of Princess Sanyukta, daughter of Jaichand, the ruler of Kanauj. The princess and Prithviraj fell in love with each other but Jaichand, who was a rival of Prithviraj, took a dim view of this romance. He refused to invite Prithviraj Chauhan to the *swayamvara* of his daughter—a ceremony at which Rajput princesses chose their husbands by garlanding the suitor of their choice. To further insult the ruler of Delhi and Ajmer, Jaichand put a statue of Prithviraj at the postern. Sanyukta was undeterred. She went down the line of suitors until she came to the statue and garlanded it. The popular romantic version of this tale says that even as she did so, she found herself swept onto a horse and carried away by Prithviraj, who had come uninvited to the ceremony.

The incident further embittered Jaichand against his Chauhan rival, and when a new wave of Turkish invaders—the Ghoris—appeared on the horizon at the end of the twelfth century, Jaichand refused to align himself with Prithviraj. With the support of a few other Rajput princes, Prithviraj marched to oppose Ghori, at the head of an army of 200,000 horses and 3,000 elephants. The Rajputs fought fiercely and succeeded in overpowering the invaders. But Ghori would not accept defeat. He returned the following year with a stronger army. This time the Rajputs were defeated, and Prithviraj was captured and put to death. With this, the Chauhan supremacy over Delhi and Ajmer ended, and the two cities were never again to be effectively recovered by the Rajputs. From the sixteenth century till the advent of the British in India, the Moghul dynasty was to flourish here. Ghori was followed by a Turk called Qutbuddin Aibak who garrisoned Ajmer—a city that opened up routes from the north to south-west and south-east Rajputana.

The reign of Allauddin Khilji, described variously as a Pathan and a Turk, saw the rapid expansion of Muslim dominion over different parts of India between the thirteenth and fourteenth centuries. The wonderful fort of Ranthambhor, on the eastern border of what is now Jaipur district, was a challenge to Khilji. Reduced by earlier conquerors, it had however been recovered by the Rajputs and was then held by a brave Rajput chief called Hamir Deva. Determined to chastise him, Khilji marched in person on Ranthambhor. It fell after a year-long siege, and Hamir Deva was killed. Records a contemporary Muslim historian: "One night the Rai lit a fire at the top of the hill, and threw his women and family into the flames, and rushing on the enemy with a few devoted adherents sacrificed his life in despair."

Allauddin followed up this victory with an attack on Mewar, the land of the brave Sisodias. It would be logical to assume that this expedition was also prompted by the desire for territorial expansion, but the famous legend about Allaudin's infatuation with Padmini, the exquisite wife of the regent of Chittor, cannot be ignored (see chapter on Udaipur and Chittor). However, no contemporary chronicle or inscription has explicitly recorded this as the reason for Allauddin's conquest. The fortress of Chittor also fell to Khilji despite a desperate resistance.

Khilji and subsequent conquerors were to discover that their victories on the soil of Rajputana were difficult to achieve and to consolidate. The terrain and the Rajput genius for building fortresses on the broad tops of scarped hills made it difficult to gain a foothold there. Moreover, the Rajputs had learnt from the aboriginal tribes native to the Aravallis, guerrilla methods of resisting aggression.

The sixteenth century saw a revival of Rajput strength. Rebellion was taking a toll of the last Afghan dynasty at Delhi, and Malwa and Gujarat, under Muslim rulers, were at war with each other. In Mewar, at this time, rose a Sisodia chief called Rana Sangram Singh, to be immortalised in chronicles and legends as Rana Sanga. A man endowed with remarkable military prowess, he succeeded in enlarging the borders of Mewar and regaining for his clan some extent of the supremacy they had enjoyed in central India. He fought successfully against Malwa, Delhi and Gujarat, and organized the financial resources and the military forces of Mewar in a concerted bid to rebuild Rajput supremacy following the break-up of the Delhi Sultanate.

Sanga was the battle-scarred veteran of a hundred fields. Colonel James Tod, in his work *Annals and Antiquities of Rajasthan*, draws a vivid word picture of the man: "He exhibited at his death but the fragments of a warrior: one eye was lost in the broil with the Lodi King of Delhi, and he was a cripple owing to a limb being broken by a cannon-ball in another; while he counted eighty wounds from the sword or the lance on various parts of his body."

The most crucial battle of Rana Sanga's career came in 1527. Babur, a Moghul who was to establish the only lasting Muslim empire in India, took Delhi even as Sanga was setting his sights on that city. With both the Moghuls and the Rajputs trying to establish supremacy in northern India, it was inevitable that they should meet on a battlefield.

In 1527, they met at Khanua, in Bharatpur state, with Sanga leading troops representing a confederacy of Rajput clans who had united to resist the Moghuls. A great many chiefs from various provinces were slain in that battle which ended in a Rajput defeat.

The defeat at Khanua was a fatal blow to dreams of a Rajput revival. After Sanga, Mewar was crippled and unable to stand up to a subsequent attack by the Muslim Sultan of Gujarat. Chittor fell, and Malwa, the territory Rana Sanga had regained, was once again seized from the Sisodias.

In Marwar, about this time, the chief of Jodhpur, Maldeo, was proving to be the strongest ruler of his dynasty. He recovered Ajmer and gradually increased his wealth and territory. His kingdom was invaded by Sher Shah, the usurper of the throne of Delhi from Babur's successor Humayun. But though the battle was a close one,

Maldeo succeeded in forcing Sher Shah to retreat. Sher Shah's attempt to overrun Marwar had been more a matter of prestige than a strategic necessity. There was little to be gained from annexing this desert land. He is recorded to have remarked ruefully afterwards that he had hazarded his empire for a handful of barley.

Following his successful resistance of Sher Shah, Maldeo emerged as the strongest Rajput ruler of that period, and one who might have spear-headed another Rajput effort to regain supremacy. But shortly after, Babur's grandson Akbar appeared on the scene, and neither Marwar nor Mewar were to have much opportunity after that to indulge in dreams of a Rajput revival.

Akbar was the greatest Moghul of them all. He was to decisively consolidate his dynasty's empire in India. He was born in adversity, in an oasis in the Indian desert where his father Humayun had fled to after Sher Shah had driven him out of Delhi. Akbar was to prove his mettle early. He is supposed to have fought his first battle at twelve, shortly after which his father regained the throne. Humayun did not live long after, and at the age of eighteen, the youthful Emperor Akbar was able to turn his attention to the Rajputs.

He recovered Ajmer from Maldeo of Marwar and forced him to acknowledge his sovereignty. Akbar also had the sagacity to use means other than the sword to consolidate his empire. He married a Rajput princess of the Kachhwaha clan, which ruled over Amber and later Jaipur. The Kachhwaha's relationship with the Moghuls was in sharp contrast to the other Rajputs. While the house of Chittor was ready to fight unto death rather than submit to the Muslim invader, the house of Amber (Jaipur) succumbed early to Moghul supremacy. They extended to the emperors in Delhi military support and, as in the case of Akbar, gave them their daughters in marriage.

Bahar Mal, a Kachhwaha chief of the mid-sixteenth century, was the first to pay homage to Mohammedan power: he received from the Emperor Humayun the command of 5,000 horses and gave his daughter in marriage to Akbar. His successors were to follow in his footsteps. The commander-in-chief of Akbar's army was in fact the ruler of Amber, Man Singh I.

Other Rajput chiefs were also given high ranks in Akbar's armies and sent out to command distant frontiers. The only irritant was Mewar. Even after Akbar had vanquished Chittor and later defeated the Sisodia chief, Rana Pratap, in battle, the latter refused to surrender. "Has anyone seen the Maharana bow his head before the balustrade in the Moghul court?" asks a famous poem on Maharana Pratap. To the end, though sorely tempted at one stage, Rana Pratap never gave Akbar the satisfaction of receiving his submission. It was Akbar's son Jehangir, the son of a Rajput mother, who was to receive the submission of the ruler of Mewar, Pratap's successor. Then too, the submission was not made by the Rajput prince in person.

The last Moghul Emperor Aurangzeb, who was a religous bigot, succeeded in uniting the Rajputs against him. The Rathors and Sisodias, whom he thoroughly alienated, fought against him. After his death, the Rajputs, in their own defence, attempted to form a triple alliance among the three leading clans, Sisodia, Rathor and Kachhwaha. But a fatal clause in the treaty defeated its purpose. It stipulated that in the succession of the Rathor and Kachhwaha chieftainships, the son of a Sisodia princess would have preference. The disputes arising from this split up the federation.

The eighteenth century thus saw the decline of Rajputana's individual kingdoms. The quarrels over succession made these states vulnerable to attacks from the Marathas and the Muslims. Anarchy, plunder and economic ruin followed. In Tod's language, it "ended only with the total ruin and humiliation of this noble race."

The British had, in the meantime, begun to rapidly expand their dominion over the rest of the country. Like the Moghuls before them, they were quick to grasp the importance of having the Rajputs as allies, and opened negotiations with some of the Rajput states.

The anarchy following Maratha raids and their own internal dissensions had paved the way for British supremacy in Rajputana. After that, it was a matter of time before these once fiercely independent states entered into defensive alliances with the British. Between 1817 and 1823, Kotah, Udaipur, Bundi, Kishangarh (near Ajmer), Bikaner, Jaipur, Jaisalmer, Sirohi and some branches of the Udaipur house all signed such treaties, bartering away their independence in exchange for British protection.

Why were the Rajputs so consistently the victims of the territorial ambitions of others? One answer could be that they lacked both political foresight and national consciousness. It becomes clear from the wearying succession of battles that they never went far enough to break the power of an enemy, and usually pursued a purely defensive policy. They failed to take the offensive. Moreover, whenever a Rajput got an opportunity to finish off a foe, his misguided sense of chivalry usually led him to release the foe, so that he was inevitably attacked again.

Some historians also point out that the introduction of the caste system in the social polity of the Hindus made them excessively conscious of their separateness, and sapped the foundations of a common nationality. The goal of national preservation was therefore neglected.

The Rajput clans did not realize the importance of uniting effectively until it was too late. To do so would have required political foresight which they possessed in much less measure than gallantry.

After India became independent from British rule in 1947, the rulers of the princely states, including those of Rajputana acceded to the Indian Union. For the loss of their kingdoms or what remained of these, they received privy purses. These were fixed at a percentage of their annual revenue. The maharajas of yesteryears were, however, allowed to keep their palaces and personal privileges, such as gun-salutes and freedom from taxes.

In independent India, many went on to enter Parliament, the Government and the army. In 1970, the Prime Minister of India, Indira Gandhi, abolished the privy purses, thus reducing the former rulers well and truly to ordinary Indian citizens. A book on the subject records that, faced with sudden impoverishment, some maharajas found themselves in dire straits, and were reduced to selling family heirlooms. But they kept their palaces, and judiciously proceeded to convert them into luxury hotels. Udaipur, Jaipur, Jodhpur, Bharatpur and Bikaner now all offer palace hotels.

The house of Jaipur is believed to be the wealthiest as well as the most well-ordered of the princely families in Rajasthan. Its scions have gone into business and industry. The former Maharaja of Bikaner who still lives in a portion of the Lalgarh Palace Hotel, is a former Member of Parliament and a celebrated shooting champion.

Above: A view of rugged Chittor Fort.
Below: The lotus pool in the courtyard of the Lake Palace Hotel, Udaipur.

Above: Cannons on the ramparts of Jodphur Fort overlooking the city.
Below: The cenotaph of Maharaja Man Singh.

Culture and Festivals

"THE RAJPUT SLAYS BUFFALOES, HUNTS AND EATS the boar and deer, and shoots ducks and wild fowl; he worships his horse, his sword and the sun and attends more to the martial song of the bard than to the litany of the Brahmin."

In his annals, James Tod sketches a race that lived intensely, valued honour above life, and battled fiercely to hold its own against invading armies and plundering marauders. Again and again through his annals, Tod indulges in his favourite theme: the Rajputs had little in common with meek Hindus who worshipped kine and fed on fruits, herbs and water. They bore instead a compelling resemblance to ancient Germanic and Scandinavian tribes.

There is an incurable romanticism in this view for which Tod can be forgiven, because of his genuine admiration for the Rajputs. But Tod is not alone in romanticising the people of Rajasthan. Everything about them — the legends of their derring-do in battle, their exaggerated sense of honour and fidelity which drove thousands of young women to the pyre, and their innate love of beauty and colour — makes them an attractive subject.

Chivalry has become synonymous with the Rajput. There are numerous instances of their having spared foes, setting them free after capturing them, and allowing them to return home unmolested. Such generosity usually proved short-sighted.

The great warrior and statesman Maharana Kumbha of Chittor scored a victory in battle over the Sultan of the neighbouring kingdom of Malwa and took him captive. After the Sultan had remained a prisoner at Chittor for six months, he was liberated without ransom by the magnanimous Maharana. This proved to be a political folly. Several wars with Malwa followed the Sultan's release, for he made repeated attempts to wipe out his disgrace and even formed an alliance with the Sultan of Gujarat to invade Mewar.

Similarly, the great emperor of Ajmer and Delhi, Prithviraj Chauhan, successfully repulsed the invader, Sultan Shahbuddin Ghori, in the late twelfth century. The Rajput king captured his Muslim opponent, and then chivalrously allowed Ghori to return to his country. Ghori, untrammelled by notions of chivalry, invaded India again with a stronger army, attacked Prithviraj Chauhan for the second time and defeated and killed him.

There are other instances of encounters between Rajput princes and the Moghuls where the former declined to take their enemy unawares when they had the opportunity, because it went against their sense of honour. Indeed, some historians maintain that if the Rajputs had been more ruthless in suppressing their foes, they would have spared Rajputana a good many wars and ensured their kingdoms' greater stability.

Closely associated with the Rajputs is their willingness to battle unto death rather than surrender, and the zealous guarding of the honour of their wives and women. *Sati*, that gruesome Hindu custom of wives burning on their husbands' pyres, was not confined to Rajasthan, but it was performed here in horrifyingly large numbers. Six wives and fifty-eight concubines are said to have accompanied Ajit Singh of Marwar to the funeral pyre. And no less than sixty-eight committed the rite at the funeral of Raja Budh Singh of Bundi. In such cases, the chief queen had the privilege of being burnt with the corpse, while the others performed the rite in separate fires. *Sati* was most prevalent in the houses of Mewar, Marwar, Jaipur and Bikaner. It was not confined to the princely houses but extended to the higher castes of the Hindu hierarchy (Brahmins, Rajputs, Charans) associated with the ruling houses. The peasant and trader classes seldom practised it.

One vivid description of the ritual records that the widow, richly attired and covered with costly jewels and ornaments, mounted a gorgeously caparisoned horse. As the procession moved on, she unclasped her ornaments one by one and flung them to the crowd until she reached the pyre shorn of her jewels.

Satis are commemorated in Rajasthan by tablets with women's handprints engraved on them. These are found in forts and palaces all over the state.

Another gruesome rite, *jauhar*, was probably confined to

Rajasthan alone. *Jauhar* was the ritual of mass suicide in anticipation of capture by an enemy. From the battlefield, a sign would be given to the families within the fortress, to indicate defeat or victory. If it was the former, all the women in the stronghold would enter a chamber where a fire had been kept burning, and immolate themselves.

There is a bizarre tale of one such occasion when by mistake, the wrong flag was raised, signalling defeat instead of victory. By the time the victors returned to the palace, they found it empty — the *jauhar* had already taken place.

Rajput men also abhorred capture. When defeat seemed certain, they would don saffron robes and hurl themselves at the enemy, determined to fight to death.

Another kind of ritual killing remorselessly observed was female infanticide. For a girl to be unmarried was a disgrace and yet, finding a suitable match became more and more difficult as a complicated system of preventing inter-clan marriages evolved. Also, in those days, dowries were very elaborate affairs among the Rajputs and those who could not afford these preferred to kill a female child as soon as she was born.

The Rajputs meticulously observed rites concerning war, marriage and the numerous religious ceremonies that clutter up the life of the Hindu. Hinduism with its various sects flourished in Rajasthan; and so did Jainism, the latter being tolerated because it was the religion of wealthy merchants and traders. Many notable examples of Jain temple architecture can still be found in Rajasthan.

The usual Hindu festivals of Deepavali, the festival of lights, and Holi, the festival of colour, have always been celebrated here with verve and zest. But Rajasthan has a couple of others that are typically its own.

Gangaur, dedicated to Gauri or Parvati, the consort of Lord Shiva, begins on the day after Holi and lasts eighteen days. It is a festival when married women pray for their husbands. Tod's annals describe the traditional rites associated with this festival. "The rituals commence, when the sun enters Aries, with a deputation to a spot beyond the city to bring earth for the image of Gauri. When this is formed, a smaller one of Iswara is made, and they are placed together. A small trench is then excavated in which barley is sown; the ground is irrigated till the grain germinates, when the females join hands and dance around it. After that, apparently, the young corn is plucked and presented by the women to the men who wear it in their turbans." On the final day, the goddess and her consort are given a ceremonial bath.

Another occasion for women to congregate, dress gaily and worship is Teej, the swing festival, which usually comes in August. Teej, too, is dedicated to Parvati, celebrating the day when she was reunited with Shiva after long "austerities" (Tod). Girls and women take turns on gaily decorated swings, singing traditional songs as they swing to and fro.

Raksha Bandhan or Rakhi is also celebrated in the same month. Girls and women tie bracelets called *rakhis* on the right wrists of men, usually their brothers, thereby seeking their protection, which the men are enjoined to give.

There is a moving story concerning the Emperor Humayun and Princess Karnavati of Chittor. During the sack of Chittor by the Sultan of Gujarat, the princess sent a *rakhi* to Humayun, thereby making him her brother, and uncle and protector to her infant son Udai Singh. She herself died in a *jauhar* before Humayun could come to her rescue, but it is recorded that Humayun "amply fulfilled his pledge" and expelled the foe from Chittor.

Today's *rakhis* are creations of tinsel and coloured paper or plastic. But in the days of yore, it could be of "flock silk and spangles or gold chain and gems," depending on the means and rank of the donor.

Apart from festivals, there are a great many fairs in Rajasthan's calendar. There is the Pushkar fair, a mammoth five-day gathering of devotees at the Pushkar Lake, where they worship and bathe in observance of Kartik Purnima, the autumn full moon (*see chapter on* Ajmer). The grounds where the people camp to sell and buy camels, cattle and goods are a sea of multi-coloured turbans — orange, yellow, red. The women wear gay *bandhani* (tie-and-dye) skirts, veils and saris, and plenty of chunky silver jewellery. Bonfires are lit, and dances and music enliven the fair grounds.

There are other less important fairs marking the births and deaths of saints, honouring the snake god, and local heroes. If they did not have an occasion, the village folk would invent one, for celebration is a vital, joyous instinct in the Rajasthani.

No wonder then that there are so many balladeers and minstrels wandering from village to village, drawing crowds spontaneously. Some of them, such as the Bhatts and Charans, are castes of hereditary bards which have handed down their repertoires of heroic verses and folklore from father to son. They perform at every festival to a rapt crowd of listeners.

So do the ballad singers, and in desert Rajasthan their folk songs, often rendered in the rich tenor of a practised minstrel, are tremendously evocative. A class of balladeers who are always a big draw are the *padh* singers. A *padh* is a long, painted curtain on which are depicted episodes in the life of a folk hero of Marwar, called Pabuji. Pabuji was an ally of Rao Jodha who founded Jodhpur. The singer dwells on each of these episodes, accompanying his singing on a stringed instrument and bow. His wife, her face always covered by the sari or veil, carries a lamp with which she illuminates the relevant episode on the painted curtain while her husband sings.

Rajasthan's wealth of legends finds myriad means of expression. When the balladeer, bard and minstrel have had their turn, folk theatre and puppet theatre take over, harmoniously mixing music, dance, mime and dialogue.

Then there are the dances: swinging folk-dances such as the *ghummar*; trick dances such as *tera tali*, in which the woman precariously balances swords while onlookers hold their breath; and gay Stick Dances. All of this can be seen at any of the festivals that the Department of Tourism organizes: the desert festival at Jaisalmer, the summer festival at Abu, and the special shows at Pushkar.

Above: Handprints in stone to commemorate *satis*. These are found all over Rajasthan.

Facing page
Top: Young brides-to-be on a Jodhpur street.

Bottom: A marriage procession in Jaipur.

Above left: The cobra deity, Vasajnoj, with his two queens.
Above right: A village shrine dedicated to the monkey god, Hanuman.

Facing page
Top: A village depiction of Tejaji, a folk deity. This much loved legend is about a man who tried to save a serpent from a fire, and earned a bite for his kindness.
Bottom left: The image of Tejaji in the Udaipur Museum of Folk Art.
Bottom right: Two other folk deities, Goraji and Kalaji (literally, the black man and the white man).

Above: Puppets in Jaipur.
Left: A *padh* singer, one of a tribe of balladeers who narrate a tale illustrated in the long painted curtain.

33

Left: The *tera tali* dance.
Below left: The Fire Dance, performed on burning embers.
Below right: A dancer performs the Bhavainritya, a dance in which the performer balances several earthern vessels on her head. She herself balances on glass tumblers.

Facing page
Top: Rajasthan's Stick Dance.
Below: Musicians accompanying the dancers.

Above: Intricate *mehndi* or henna leaf-dyed designs adorn the palms of Rajasthani women for festivals and weddings.
Below: Bathing in Pushkar Lake during the annual festival of Kartik Purnima.

Geography and Wild Life

In Rajasthani, Aravalli means "a beam lying across". It is an appropriate name for a mountain range that stretches across the state from north-east to south-west. Its hills and ravines form a natural divide between two river systems and two different kinds of terrain. It is in Rajasthan that the desert belt, girding half the world, merges into India's rain-fed centre. On the west, there is dune and scrub, but as you travel eastwards, towards Jaipur from Jaisalmer and Jodhpur, it gradually gives way to a greater proportion of cultivated green. Once the rains come, the hills surrounding Jaipur turn green.

To the south-east of Jaipur is a plateau drained by the Chambal River and its tributaries. It is volcanic in origin, a wide, stony upland with occasional tracts of deep black soil in the river valleys. The local name for this region has long been "Pathar", or stone.

The desert is perhaps the most striking feature of Rajasthan's geography. No other state in the country has such a relentless spread of scrub and cactus. The local name for this region, "Marusthali" or land of death, is sufficiently evocative: little grows here, and except for the camel, desert fox and swarms of locusts, even fauna is rare. Summers are scorching, winters cold, and rain scarce.

The Thar desert forms part of the desert belt extending from the Sahara in north Africa, across Arabia to the west and north-west of Rajasthan, its furthest extremity being the Great Gobi of Central Asia. The Thar makes up part of the country's boundary. For about seven hundred miles, Rajasthan faces Pakistan across the Thar, which stretches well into that country.

In the south-western corner of the state, where the Aravallis have their highest point in the hills around Mount Abu, the vegetation is in sharp contrast to the desert, north of here. Rajasthan's only hill resort is set in lush green sub-tropical forest, with flowering shrubs growing wild. The hills are fairly high here, the ravines surrounding them are thickly vegetated, and birds abound. Part of the region forms a sanctuary for the leopard, sambar, chital and chinkara.

James Tod, in his monumental treatise on Rajasthan's life and legends, credits himself with being the first to put together a reliable map of Rajasthan, in 1815. It was a feat which involved marching at midnight and surviving raids by plundering dacoits. Tod was a diligent surveyor, criss-crossing Rajputana, tracing rivers to their source, pushing through untrodden fields and sending out survey parties to map regions he could not personally penetrate.

Apart from the Aravallis, part of another central Indian hill range is in Rajasthan, the Vindhyas. This makes southernmost Rajasthan hilly too, and for tribes who live here in scattered hamlets, only one crop a year is possible. Before the monsoon, there is dry stubble but once the rains come maize, the hardiest crop in this region, sprouts everywhere.

Rajasthan's geography has influenced both its history and its economy. Both the Aravallis and the Vindhyas have sheltered tribes like the Bhils and Mers, who were the original inhabitants of Rajputana. The terrain encouraged them to develop guerrilla methods of warfare which bewildered Muslim invaders. The Rajputs who were later to settle in and rule over this region, were quick to master these tactics.

If successive invaders were not able to gain a strong foothold in the Rajput states, it was largely because of the terrain. The rugged ravines and valleys of the Aravallis enabled the local rulers to hold out against Moghul enemies despite heavy odds. For instance, when Emperor Akbar invaded Chittor in 1569, Rana Udai Singh (who founded Udaipur) slipped away into the hills where he remained untraced by the enemy.

Rajasthan's rivers have also helped to shape the course of events. The Chambal River has admitted into Rajasthan a long list of settlers and invaders covering the period from the early Aryan to the Turkish and Moghul. Also, the early Aryans, in their gradual dispersion over north-western India are thought to have reached the Arabian Sea via the tributaries of the Luni River. The Luni is the only river of consequence in this part of the country and rises in

Lake Pushkar near Ajmer, an important place of pilgrimage, where a huge fair is held each year. The Luni then flows south-west to India's great salt marsh in the neighbouring state of Gujarat, and then into the sea.

If the barrenness of the land does not lend itself to agricultural wealth, it fortunately yields substantial mineral wealth. Mines scar the countryside, yielding not only the more plebeian industrial ores such as gypsum, mica, copper and tungsten, but also the country's only emerald, and its finest marble.

Makrana, a small town in Nagaur district, has become a synonym for quality marble: slabs quarried from it centuries ago built the Taj Mahal in Agra, and later the Victoria Memorial in Calcutta. Each year, production increases with demand, varying from both coarse and finely grained white marble to beds of pink marble in Kala Dhungri. There are over 200 quarries scattered over the low marble-bearing hills, and almost the entire population of the town makes a living out of marble.

Mewar's silver mines feed jewellers' shops in Jaipur, Udaipur and nearby Nathdwara, where the famous enamel work on silver, called *meenakari*, has its home.

The mineral wealth of the Aravallis once enhanced the personal revenues of the princes of this region. Tod records that the chieftain of Salumbar coined his copper currency from the mines on his own estate.

The princes and chieftains of the erstwhile kingdoms of Rajasthan not only found their wealth in their own backyards but their leisure as well. The royal hunts, which were indulged in with savage glee, necessitated shooting preserves for each of these families. Most of the sanctuaries that dot the state today have their origin in these preserves.

The tiger, leopard, deer, sambar, wild boar and blackbuck, which constitute the state's fast diminishing wild life, were once captive prey for Rajput spring hunts. The sovereign, his sons and chieftains set out on steeds over hills and ravines and through jungle coverts, bearing lances with which they hoped to impale wild boar.

Tiger shooting was the most sophisticated pastime of the rulers of Jaipur. The sixty square miles of low outcrop hills which now constitute the Sawai Madhopur sanctuary were once famous for tiger hunts. Lesser sanctuaries are now found scattered over southern and eastern Rajasthan.

But the state's largest collections of wild life are found at Bharatpur and Sariska. In season, Bharatpur's swampy marsh is so chockful of birds that the trees are white with droppings and the air filled with bird cries. Flamingoes, pelicans and the Siberian cranes fly here in winter to breed, and between October and February there is a great deal of noisy, feathery activity.

Sariska's tigers are a lot more elusive than the birds, but they do occasionally oblige visitors perched in the two watch-towers at this sanctuary, by coming down to the water-holes. Sariska, approximately twenty-five miles from Alwar, was once a shooting preserve of the rulers of Alwar. Poaching is a bit of a menace here, but then poaching in Rajasthan has royal antecedents: the grand hunts of Prithviraj Chauhan, once ruler of Delhi, are recorded to have often led him into warfare, for he was a poacher of the first magnitude.

Rajasthan has begun to attract the attention of conservationists rather late. The Indian lion became extinct from this state in the latter half of the last century, and the cheetah disappeared from here at the turn of the present. More recently, there has been an outcry over a royal Saudi Arabian hunting party coming to shoot the Great Indian Bustard, a large ostrich-like ground bird that totters on the brink of extinction in the Jaisalmer area.

The climate varies across the state. While it is searing hot in Jodhpur, Jaisalmer and Bikaner in the summer months, it is delightfully pleasant in Abu, south of this area. The best season to visit the desert cities is winter and the ideal time to be in Udaipur and Jaipur is from just after the rains in September-October to the following February.

Top: Sunrise at Pushkar.
Below: Sand dunes at dusk.

Above: Sunset in the desert.
Left: Clambering onto an indignant camel in Pushkar.

Facing page
Top: A shepherd with his flock of goats.
Below: In the fields.

Above: A painted stork flies over the marsh.
Below: Sarus cranes frolic in the reeds.

Art and Architecture

A RAJPUT HUNTER REACHES FOR HIS SWORD AS HIS steed catches up with a boar, even as his racing hound sinks its teeth into the animal's flank. The Lord Krishna dances to the music of two damsels. A woman mystic, holding her musical instrument, communes with deer in a forest. A bejewelled lady of leisure waters flowering plants on her terrace while her peacock is immobilised by an approaching snake. Another woman holds her cloak off, as she preens in the nude before a mirror held by a handmaiden.

There was nothing dull or squeamish about Rajasthan's miniature painters. Their paintings are bold, alive and exquisite in detail. Fortunately, because of a royal tradition which encouraged patronage of art, Rajasthan has a wealth of miniatures as almost every princely state developed a school of its own.

Art, in Rajasthan, falls into three categories. There were paintings made for feudal patrons depicting court grandeur, hunting scenes, processions, expeditions, battles and romantic episodes based on contemporary literature. Then there was a more popular kind of art based on folklore and folk art, meant for those who bought portraits of gods on religious and festive occasions, either for worship or for decoration. Brightly coloured *pichwais*, or folk paintings, with red and yellow as the dominant colours, fall in this category. These are still widely available.

The third category of paintings was done in manuscript form or on cloth, based on literature or mythology. *Padh* paintings, which formed the basis for verses sung by *padh* singers (see chapter on Culture and Festivals), were of this kind.

Miniature painting in Rajasthan falls in the first category and was influenced by the Gujarat and Moghul schools. Several distinct schools of Rajasthan miniatures emerged: the Mewar or Udaipur school, the Bundi school, the Kishangarh school, the Bikaner school, the Jaipur school and the Alwar school. Towards the turn of the nineteenth century, artists in Kotah distinguished themselves with paintings of a novel style and character, of which more later.

The earliest of these was the Mewar school. During the reign of Rana Pratap Singh's son, Amar Singh I, early in the seventeenth century, a series of paintings, most of which are now in a private collection, were done at Chavand, a village south of Udaipur. These are considered valuable for their distinct style. A comparison of this particular series with later paintings done in Mewar, during the Muslim emperor Jehangir's reign, demonstrates the nature of the impact which submission to the Moghuls made on the artists in Mewar. The later paintings were bright, had clear colours and were more naturalistic than the earlier ones with stylised trees, hills, rocks and water used in pattern formation. Human figures in the Mewar school have a prominent nose, oval face and fish-shaped eyes.

The most important school of painting in Rajasthan developed in the eighteenth century in the state of Kishangarh. Kishangarh lies between Jaipur and Ajmer, and was founded by Kishan Singh of the Jodhpur house. A descendant of this house, Prince Sawant Singh, is the personality around whom the Kishangarh paintings centre. He was a devotee of Lord Krishna and abdicated his throne to spend the rest of his life at Brindaban (Krishna's birth-place, near Mathura) in the worship of the Lord. Sawant Singh's other passion in life was a lovely singer called Bani Thani, who became his mistress. These two passions inspired a wonderful group of pictures painted during his period.

The artists of the Kishangarh school invented a new and beautiful stylisation for the divine lovers, Radha and Krishna. The features are fine but proportionate, not exaggerated, in both male and female depictions. Bani Thani is thought to have been the model for the features depicted in these paintings.

Another famous school developed at Bundi, in eastern Rajasthan. Hunting, palace and toilette scenes were popular and imbued with a certain sense of gaiety. In the last quarter of the eighteenth century, the Bundi artists produced a fairly small group of paintings labelled by some art historians as "white" paintings. In these, more than half the surface is left white, with one or two figures placed against it in low-key colours, with a few touches of red and gold. The Bundi artists were particularly fond of toilette scenes in which youthful nudes posed provocatively before a spectator.

In the second half of the seventeenth century, during the reign of the puritan Moghul Emperor Aurangzeb, patronage of art at Delhi began to decline. Many artists, therefore, moved gradually to the Rajput courts. In Bikaner, for instance, the local style was almost submerged by the close association of its ruler with the Moghul courts. Two kinds of influences are very strong in this school: the Moghul, and that of the Deccan, the region south of central India's mountain range, the Vindhyas. The rulers of Bikaner often commanded imperial armies under the Moghuls in the Deccan and elsewhere, and sometimes brought back artists from these regions or acquired many paintings during their military expeditions.

The Jaipur school, too, given this dynasty's history of cooperation with the Moghuls, was heavily influenced by the Moghul artists. The practice of portraiture was learnt from the Moghul court. Portraiture and court scenes predominate, and the latter are liberally embellished with gold.

At the turn of the nineteenth century, Kotah produced a refreshingly different body of paintings celebrating the chase. Hunting, particularly tiger hunting, was depicted in the hilly jungles of Kotah, amid thickets of bamboo. The rendering is natural rather than stylised. The hunters are often reduced to heads peering intently through leaves. The pictures effectively convey the excitement of nights in the silent jungle.

Apart from miniatures, mural painting was also a practised art. The common people, during weddings, adorned the walls outside their houses with bright folk designs, depicting horses, elephants, and people. In palace chambers, court painters produced more formal murals, elaborate wall paintings in the same style as the miniatures.

If Rajasthan's art is fascinating, its architecture is, quite simply, spectacular. Nothing recalls its history as effectively as its marvellous forts astride broad, scarped hills. And nowhere else in India are there Jain temples as celebrated as those in Rajasthan.

The Rajputs were great builders, and when they borrowed ideas they did so tastefully. They borrowed from the Muslims the art of filigreeing marble and sandstone and introduced it in their palaces and *havelis* (traditionally designed houses). And though they continued, as good Hindus, to cremate their dead, they are thought to have picked up from the Moghuls the art of sepulchral adornment. Hence the cenotaphs on the outskirts of practically every city of Rajputana.

Cenotaphs, palaces, forts and temples abound in Rajasthan, giving it perhaps a richer architectural heritage than any other single state in the country. Victory towers, though fewer in number, offer an equally impressive visual spectacle. The large artificial lake locally known as *samand* or sea, is another form in which the Rajput artistic genius found expression.

The Rajputs built hundreds of forts (known as *garhs*), with Mewar's illustrious fifteenth-century statesman Rana Kumbha setting the pace. According to his contemporary writers, he built more than thirty-two fortresses, with reservoirs, palaces, temples and houses for the common folk within the surrounding walls and battlements.

The profusion of fortresses, in one sense, is an indication of the times, for frequent invasions and counter-invasions marked the attempts at territorial expansion. Forts were built to hold down the conquered country and to keep the people in subjugation, as well as to protect and secure a town against invaders.

Architects of the period have described the principles on which the fortresses were generally planned. For the safety of the inhabitants, these were to be constructed on a high cliff, protected by bastions and gates, and guarded by an armed force. They were to be amply provided with wells, tanks and pools, as well as agricultural land, so as to be able to hold out during long sieges.

In keeping with these requirements, the sites of Chittor, Ranthambor and Kumbhalgarh forts were chosen on inaccessible precipices. Walls were constructed in several concentric rows, and wide moats dug. But, for all this, the military architects of the times were short-sighted enough to ignore the danger presented by neighbouring mounds. The hillock of Chitori near Chittorgarh enabled Bahadur Shah and Akbar to station artillery there and break up the defence of that fort. And the fort of Kumbhalgarh was vulnerable to external assault because the projecting cliffs all around it gave protection to the enemy from arrows shot from the parapets, and frustrated the rolling down of stones from above. At regular intervals along the walls of some forts, such as Jaisalmer, massive stone balls can still be seen. These were pushed down onto advancing enemy forces.

Royal residences inside fortresses were usually constructed with narrow and secret passages for escape during a siege. Many of these have now been walled up.

Rajput palaces with their halls for public and private audiences — *Diwan-i-am* and *Diwan-i-khas* — their fountains, slender columns and gardens reflect the influence of the Moghul style. But in the imagery employed in the murals and other decorations, the artists were able to indulge in an abundant display of animal and human figures. James Ferguson, in *Indian and Eastern Architecture*, notes: "There (at Fatehpur Sikri) the Muslims' antipathy to images confined the fancy of the decorator to purely inanimate objects, here (at Amber palace) the later creed of the Hindus enable him to indulge in elephant capitals and figure sculpture of men and animals to any extent."

The Rajputs also picked up the art of inlaid-mirror work from the Moghuls. The palaces at Jaipur and Udaipur have borrowed the idea of a *Sheesh Mahal*, or hall of mirrors, from older palaces at Delhi and Agra. Udaipur's city palace is perhaps one of the most richly embellished of Rajput royal residences, with enamelled peacocks, mirror-work, Chinese tiles, sculpture and murals adorning its many sections. It also has a garden in its upper storeys, and overhangs a lake.

Several Rajput palaces were thus situated, overlooking an artificial lake or pool, or in the midst of one. This is true of those at Amber, Bundi and Udaipur, and of Padmini's palace at Chittorgarh. The Deeg palaces, too, look out on one side on to a large tank and, in front, they face fountains and water channels set in a lovely, formal sunken garden laid out in the Moghul style.

Chhatri, literally meaning 'umbrella', is the local name for cenotaphs, found on the outskirts of practically every town the Rajputs built. The capital of every state in Rajputana has its *mahasati*, the place where the sovereigns of the state and their nearest relations are cremated, which is located at a secluded spot, a little way from the town. The word *chhatri* appropriately describes these cenotaphs, for the usual style was to have a domed canopy supported by columns.

Udaipur has a very large number of these, ranging from simple four-columned ones to far more elaborate structures. The cenotaph of Sangram Singh II who, in the eighteenth century, was cremated at that spot with twenty-one of his wives, is a particularly fine specimen. It has a fifty-six-pillared portico with an octagonal dome in the centre. The dome itself is supported by eight dwarf pillars.

Further north in Rajasthan, the Hindus adopted quite a different style in their palaces and cenotaphs. The foliated arch, common in the Moghul palaces of Agra and Delhi, can be seen in the tomb of Bakhtawar Singh in Alwar. Erected about 1815, it has curved cornices, and several domes and pavilions. The *chhatris* of the Maharajas of Bharatpur, at a place called Goverdhan, are similar to this.

Rajasthan also has a tremendous wealth of temple architecture to offer. Some of the most splendid Jain temples in the country are found at Ranakpur and Abu, and there are other fine specimens at Jaisalmer and Lodurva. All these date between the eleventh and the fifteenth centuries. The earliest temples built by this community, that are still in good shape, are at Osian, a village some thirty miles from Jodhpur.

The Jain community in Rajasthan was, and still is, a prosperous trader class which formed the backbone of the local economy. For this reason, most rulers gave them freedom of worship. The Jains expressed their devotion to their faith through lavishly sculptured temples, often built in fine marble. Many of these temples were also store-houses of illustrated manuscripts and treatises.

The Jains worship no deity but follow the teachings of their twenty-four *tirthankars*, or saints, who are believed to have achieved *nirvana*, or release from material desires, in their lifetime. They also enshrine these saints in their temples, which are usually dedicated to the more important ones. Indeed, it appears to the lay observer that the Jains seek to honour these saints by the number of their images, for these are repeated tirelessly in most temples, with each principal image given a separate niche or, if space permits, a separate chapel. In the temple of Vimala at Mount Abu, there are fifty-two chapels, each containing the image of a *tirthankar*. The inner sanctum in these temples usually contains the image of the saint the temple is dedicated to. These images are generally highly stylised, showing the *tirthankar* in a position of meditation, crosslegged in the lotus position with hands folded in the lap. The statues are white, yellow or black, occasionally red. Each saint has his emblem, such as the sign of the bull for Adinath, the first *tirthankar*, and the sign of the lion for Mahavira, the last and the best known of the twenty-four.

There are two main sects among the Jains — the Svetambaras who minister to the laity, and the Digambaras who are ascetics. Sculptures of the former depict them as white-robed, while the latter are shown naked.

Hindu temples dedicated to one of the three deities in the Hindu trinity — Brahma the creator, Vishnu the preserver, and Shiva the destroyer — are also scattered all over Rajasthan. A beautiful Hindu temple of considerable antiquity, built in the classical late Gupta style, is located at Baroli in the former state of Udaipur.

The tiny village of Osian is of considerable architectural importance. It has about sixteen Brahminical and Jain temples built between the eighth and twelfth centuries, many now in a dilapidated condition. Osian was once an important centre of the Hindu and Jain religions.

The temples in Osian are in two clusters. The first group of eleven temples is in the outskirts of the village, while the other group is on a hill a little to the east. The larger group of temples belong to an earlier period, having been built in the eighth and ninth centuries. They are small temples with high plinths, and display a striking variety of designs. Some of these are of the *panchayatana* class, that is, they have five shrines, a main one and four subsidiary ones. There is also a sun temple at Osian, with two tall, fluted pillars at the entrance.

One of these Jain temples here offers a valuable opportunity to trace the style of architecture as it evolved over four centuries. It appears to have been first built in the eighth century, and repaired and added to in the tenth. The *toran*, or entrance archway, with carvings of nymphs on it, appears to be an even later addition, probably eleventh century.

The doorways of the Osian group of temples, particularly those which lead to the shrine, are quite remarkable for their abundance of carved imagery. Percy Brown, in his *Indian Architecture (Buddhist and Hindu Period)*, writes: "The fact that the shrine entrance led immediately to the divine presence seems to have given wing to the artist's imagination, so that here we find portrayed, by symbol and image, whole volumes of folklore and mythology for those who can see but cannot read."

Facing page
Top left: Folk murals of a horse and elephant on either side of the door adorn many of the homes in Udaipur.
Top right: An inlaid mural in Chini Chitrashala, Udaipur City Palace.
Bottom: Stone filigree in the palaces within Jaisalmer's "golden fortress".

Below: A miniature of the Lord Krishna on display in the Ram Nivas Bagh Museum, Jaipur.

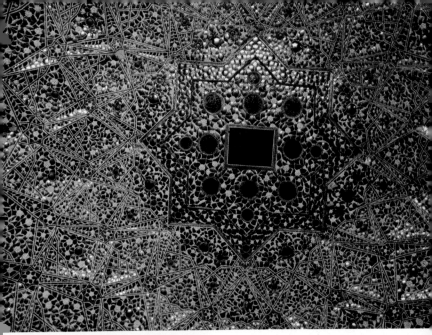

Above left: A devotee outside the portals of a Jain temple in Jaisalmer Fort.

Above: Jai Mandir's mirror-studded ceiling.

Far left: Ornate glass and mirror decorations on a wall in the Lake Palace Hotel, Udaipur.

Left: Detail of a wall decoration in Jaipur's City Palace.

Above: An ornate wall with stained-glass and inlaid-work in Jai Mandir, Amber.
Below: Cenotaphs at Mandore.

Rooftop view of the spires and cupolas of the Chaumukha Jain Temple at Ranakpur.

A view of the Maharani suite in the Lake Palace Hotel, Udaipur.

Handicrafts

IN AN OLD MUSLIM QUARTER OF BIKANER, YOUNG girls trickle into a house in the neighbourhood each afternoon for a literacy class. Usually, each one of them brings to the class, along with her books, a piece of cloth. Throughout the lesson, nimble fingers work away at the first stage of the tie-and-dye process, knotting the cloth into designs that will emerge once the cloth is dyed. Their spelling may be shaky, but their craftsmanship is practised, for children in many rural and urban localities of Rajasthan learn the craft that is a family tradition long before they learn anything else.

Bandhani, the local name for tie-resist-dyeing, is a popular heritage, said to be symbolic of girlhood, love and marital happiness, and is figured constantly in love lyrics and folk songs. Done in muslin, cotton or silk, it is widely used by women in both cities and villages as a sari or as a *dupatta*, or veil, which women drape over their embroidered skirts, called *ghagras*.

There are two methods of doing tie-and-dye. In one, the draughtsman divides the whole surface of the cloth into one-inch squares. It is then given to the knotter, usually a young girl, who picks up a little cloth at each corner of the squares, and ties it into a knot with pack-thread, the number and position of the knots being decided by the pattern that the cloth is to take. With a different kind of knotting, a striped variation called *lahariya* (literally meaning 'ripples') is produced. The cloth is then dyed in the chosen colour. The knots prevent the tied up parts from being dyed, thus leaving them uncoloured.

In the other method, the cloth is fastened on to a wooden block with pins set in the required design and the raised points are tied with waxed string.

Handicrafts are as integral a part of Rajasthan's heritage as its deserts and ravines and its folklore. The variety that can be found outdoes every other state in the country. Apart from tie-and-dye, there is printing with silver and gold on cloth, enamelling on gold, silver and glass, gem-cutting, engraving of iron, steel, brass and copper, and carpet-making. Carpets in Jaipur and Bikaner are often produced in the jails. Craftsmen in Rajasthan's villages and in the old, traditional quarters of its cities also fashion stoneware in polished marble, ornaments of shellac and lacquer, and jewellery in silver and gold. Ivory and wood carving, pottery, handmade paper, and camel-hide work also figure in the seemingly endless series of crafts.

An old British resident of Jaipur has recorded elaborate notes on some of the crafts which flourished in Rajasthan and which assumed the proportions of an industry. One of these was the art of miniature painting, which was done on card, thick paper, or gold-beater's skin. Large quantities of brightly coloured pictures, of every grade of merit, were produced throughout the state. For the best artists, it was an amazingly lucrative profession. In Jaipur, some of them were employed by the royal family, receiving retaining fees in the shape of salaries or lands, with the privilege of working for private parties when not wanted in the palace. Where the son was gifted, these posts became hereditary.

Patronage of this art was so widespread all over the state that almost every noble had a painter in his retinue, and in the towns were several middlemen who dealt solely in pictures. The subjects of these decorations were predictable, and reflected popular demand: you could buy a series depicting the various incarnations of deities such as Vishnu or Shiva, or the Goddess Durga in her various forms, or illustrations of the Sikh gurus or the Jain lords. In Jaipur, records our British Resident, you could buy portraits of the local maharajas, past and present, or a series of paintings depicting the ceremonies performed at every stage of a Rajput's career.

British influence made itself interestingly felt. "The most advanced artists have taken to clothing the gods in European costume with similar surroundings: thus Shiva, the Great Destroying Principle of the Hindu trinity, is shewn sitting in a hall lighted by candles in glass shades, and Krishna drives a phaeton which is filled by his friends and attendants."

Meenakari, or the art of enamelling on gold and silver, is an exquisite craft still practised in the town of Nathdwara, near Udaipur, and in Jaipur. The first enamel workers were brought into Rajasthan from Lahore by Maharaja Man Singh I who built Amber palace. When the capital was shifted from Amber to Jaipur, these craftsmen and their families also moved to the new capital.

The oldest example of Jaipur enamel is said to be the crutch staff on which Maharaja Man Singh leaned, when he stood before the throne of Emperor Akbar at the close of the sixteenth century. It was fifty-two inches long and composed of thirty-three cylinders of gold arranged on a central core of strong copper. Each of the gold cylinders was enamelled with figures of animals, landscapes and flowers.

The colours for enamelling used to be obtained from opaque vitreous masses from Lahore, where they were prepared by Mohammedan bracelet makers. The base of each colour was vitreous, and the colouring matter was the oxide of a metal such as cobalt or iron. All the colours known can be applied to gold, while black, green, blue, dark yellow, red and a salmon colour can be used with silver. Only white, black and pink can be used on copper.

The Jaipur enamel is of the Champleve variety, that is, the designs are first engraved on the object to be enamelled, and the colours are then deposited in the depressions. The design was prepared by the artist, generally in the pay of the master jeweller, who also kept books of patterns from which customers could make selections.

Another graceful traditional craft handed down through the years among the families that practised it, is the production of blue pottery. The traditional designs have been adapted for more sophisticated markets so that a medium previously confined to urns, jars and pots, is now available in wall plates, jugs, mugs, vases, ash-trays and napkin rings. At Sanganer, not far from Jaipur, you can see blue pottery being made. The chief colours used are blue from the oxide of cobalt, green from the oxide of copper, and white. Some of the pottery is semi-translucent and, in addition to blue and green, other combinations have now been evolved, such as canary yellow, dark blue and brown. Some of the best pieces are hand-painted with conventional floral or arabesque patterns.

Sanganer is also the home of the gay Sanganeri prints, hand-printed textiles that are dyed with vegetable dyes and printed with wooden blocks in the courtyards of homes. To some extent, modern chemical dyes are now replacing vegetable and mineral dyes. At Sanganer, the main colour is an orange red, with yellow and blue-black floral prints. Another small, nondescript town called Bagru (also near Jaipur) has flooded the textile market at home as well as the export market with stunning circular designs printed on bed-spreads, table-cloths and clothes.

In enthusing over the heritage that makes Rajasthan a shopper's paradise, one ought not to neglect the art that gave the state its memorable architectural wealth. Udaipur, Bikaner, Jodhpur, Jaisalmer, Ajmer and Jaipur are among the chief centres of stone-carving in India, famous for their marble and sandstone work. The scarcity of timber and abundance of stone for building purposes made stonework a highly developed craft here.

Jali work, or fretwork, is supposed to have been the eastern artist's device to subdue the fierce heat of the sun while giving free access to the breeze. This delicate filigree is done in marble or sandstone, finely fretted into a network of geometrical combinations. *Jali* work was a Moghul innovation, first introduced into this country at Agra and Fatehpur Sikri. It has been used to singularly exquisite effect in the *havelis* (traditionally designed houses) in Jaisalmer. This desert town's yellow sandstone is also fashioned into a variety of decorative articles, carved and polished by local artisans. It is a vital source of employment in a sparse area where almost nothing grows.

Rajasthani women in traditional attire.

Left: Making shoes in Jodhpur.
Below left: Making drums in Jodhpur.
Below right: Puppets on display.

Facing page
Top left: A curio shop in the Lake Palace Hotel, Udaipur.
Top right: Embroidered bags on display.
Bottom left: A sampling of ornate slippers or *jootis* in Udaipur.
Bottom right: A sari shop in Jaipur's Johri Bazaar.

Above: Freshly dyed *bandhani* saris in Jaipur.

Right: A craftsman carefully repairs an elaborate marble-inlaid panel.

Jaipur and Ajmer

RAJASTHAN HAS CITIES OF MANY COLOURS BUILT
of stone from its multi-hued sandstone quarries. But Jaipur, its pink
city, has long enjoyed the most adulation. Everybody comes to
Jaipur — tourists, merchants, exporters, designers, jewellers — for
it is the capital of the state and very much the leading centre of
Rajasthan's increasingly sought-after handicraft industry.

To the tourist, it gives a quick overview of Rajasthan's charms —
marvellously picturesque fortresses nearby, several palaces, excursions, and bazaars with beautiful textiles and jewellery spilling out
of tiny shops in narrow, crowded lanes. It has elegant hotels and a
modern, expanding university campus. It is both an old and a
new city.

The rulers of Jaipur were descendants of the Kachhwaha clan
which around the twelfth and thirteenth centuries established itself
in Amber, just outside the later city of Jaipur.

The story of Jaipur city is largely the story of Sawai Jai Singh II,
who succeeded his father as ruler of Amber at the age of eleven.
His precocious repartee when presented to the Moghul emperor
Aurangzeb is supposed to have earned him the title of Sawai
(literally meaning 'one-and-a-quarter'). Aurangzeb predicted he
would measure a quarter above other rajahs.

Eventually, of course, Jai Singh II was to measure much taller
than that — he ranks as the Kachhwaha dynasty's most illustrious
ruler. He extended the state of Amber several times beyond its
original size and shifted the capital from Amber to the plains, where
he built a brand new city, Jaipur, in 1727.

The new capital quickly became a prosperous city. The eighteenth
century was a very turbulent period for northern India, and with
the Delhi-Agra-Mathura region open to attack from the Moghul
marauders in the north and the Marathas from the south, Jaipur

became a haven for traders. Money-lenders and jewellers from Delhi and Agra converged here to make it a centre of jewellery, banking and industry.

Constructed on sound principles of town planning, it was to be the first planned city of northern India. The "pinking" of Jaipur, as it were, was a much later event — the nineteenth century contribution of a successor, Maharaja Ram Singh, in honour of visiting British royalty.

Sawai Jai Singh was also a scientist and an astronomer. He had Euclid's principles and many other scientific works translated into Sanskrit, and has left to posterity a list of stars collated by himself, known as the Zeij Muhammad Shahi.

The Jantar Manter you see in Jaipur, located across from the City Palace, is one of the five observatories Jai Singh built in Jaipur, Delhi, Varanasi, Mathura and Ujjain. The one at Jaipur is the best preserved and was in fact used until quite recently. The Jaipur government used solar time for its official purposes, and this was read on a sundial in the Jantar Manter called the Samrat Yantra. A gun used to be fired from Nahargarh fort above the city as a time signal. This practice was given up only in the 1940s, when Jaipur started using Indian Standard Time.

Jai Singh claimed to have invented all the masonry instruments in the observatory. Two of his successors made minor additions to the instruments in later years.

Jai Singh outnumbered other rulers of his dynasty in less formidable pursuits as well. He is recorded to have had twenty-seven or twenty-eight wives and four concubines, the largest number possessed by any ruler of Jaipur and Amber.

Of course, wives in those days were acquired for reasons of expediency as much as indulgence. A matrimonial alliance often sealed a treaty of unity with another state against a common foe. And so it was with Jai Singh. He married a daughter of the then Maharana of Udaipur (between whose house and the rulers of Jaipur there existed traditional enmity), the terms being that a son by her would be the heir, and that in turn her father would help Jai Singh recover some of his territory taken over by Aurangzeb's successor.

Some of the clauses in the contract signed between the two are both amusing and illuminating. The Bikaner archives have a summary of the memorandum.

"Maharaja Jai Singh agrees to the following terms:

1. Whatever Maharani Ranawat would say would be acceptable to him.
2. Maharani Ranawat would enjoy more respect than all others in the *zenana*.
3. Maharaja would pass all festival nights with said Maharani.
4. Maharaja would take rest in the palace of the said Maharani after his coming back from battle.
5. Ranawatji's palanquin would be foremost in a procession."

Posterity does not record whether these were honoured!

The key clause, regarding heirship, not mentioned here, was to prove costly. After Jai Singh's death, battles over succession threw the state into turmoil and confusion, making it vulnerable to Maratha raids.

The Jats of Bharatpur, after several successful encounters with the Jaipur chief, annexed a portion of this state, and the defection of the chief of what is now Alwar further reduced the territorial limits. By the end of the century, Jaipur had fallen into great confusion, and by 1818 or so, came under the protection of the British government.

In Jaipur, as in other cities of Rajasthan, the descendants of the erstwhile ruling family still live on a part of their property, some of their palaces having been leased out to hoteliers. The Rambagh Palace Hotel, with its cream and coral façade is a particularly gracious example of such hotels. The family of the last Maharaja of Jaipur still retains a portion of the City Palace for its personal use.

This palace is within the old fortified area of the original planned city and occupies roughly one-seventh of its area. Sawai Jai Singh II built the elegant seven-storeyed Chandra Mahal in this complex. It has apartments adorned with paintings, floral bands and mirrored walls.

Adjacent to the palace walls in the old city is Jaipur's most famous attraction, Hawa Mahal, or the Palace of Winds. It belies its name for this is no airy edifice, but a delicately chiselled façade sandwiched between more prosaic buildings on a bustling thoroughfare. It is made up of small casements, each with a window, but there is nothing behind it. It is a five-tiered composition of arches and spires, pink like the rest of the buildings on the street.

There is no certain record of why it was built, only conjecture. Maharaja Sawai Pratap Singh, who built it in 1799, was a devotee of the Hindu deities Radha and Krishna. He was also a poet, and a couplet ascribed to him suggests that the building was dedicated to them. A more romantic and possibly more plausible interpretation is that it was a pavilion from which women of the royal harem could look out onto the city without being seen themselves. Rajput women observed strict *purdah*.

Apart from the Hawa Mahal, the ruins of the old town of Amber are also a favourite with visitors. Amber today consists of a palace and a fortress on an extended hill. Both the Jaigarh fortress running its crest and the palace ramparts which are spread massively across the girth of the hill are reflected in the waters of the lake below. The whole array of fortress battlements and palaces were built between the twelfth and eighteenth centuries. Amber's most famous ruler, Man Singh I, was a fierce warrior who, as commander-in-chief of Emperor Akbar's army, subjugated territories up to a thousand miles east.

The architecture of the Amber palace is thought to approach the Moghul style, with its imposing gateways, foliated arches and double pillars. The *zenana* palace here, that is, the princesses' chambers, is thought by historians to have been executed by Moghul overseers since they resemble the *zenana* in the Agra fort. However, the capitals and doorways with sculptured peacocks and elephants are supposed to be typically Rajput.

The imitation of Moghul architecture was perhaps only to be expected, since the Amber rulers had allied themselves with the Moghul emperors in Delhi.

The Jaigarh fort, above Amber palace, was, in the mid-seventeenth century, the site of a government-organized hunt for vast treasures rumoured to be buried in secret underground chambers within the fort. The treasure was never found.

There is another fortress atop the hill directly above Jaipur city. This is Nahargarh, also built by Sawai Jai Singh II. From the top of this fort the spreading lights of Jaipur city at night are an enchanting sight.

From Jaipur to Ajmer is a couple of hours' drive. Situated in a valley, the town derives its name from Ajaymaru, the 'invincible hill', crested by the Taragarh fort.

Ajmer was founded and developed in the seventh century by the Chauhan dynasty which for a short time included Delhi in its kingdom. In the twelfth century, it was supposed to have been a flourishing garden city. Chroniclers of the time were fond of eulogising Ajmer by comparing it to mythical celestial cities. "Sri Krishna's City of Dwarika looked like a humble maid before the Queen Ajmer," wrote one in a forgivable fit of hyperbole.

The invader Mohammed Ghori, however, sacked the city unceremoniously at the end of the twelfth century, and after that it passed successively into the hands of the rulers of both Marwar and Mewar. In 1556, Akbar annexed it to the Moghul empire.

Akbar was quick to gauge the strategic importance of Ajmer, which commanded the main route from the north and held the key to the conquest of Rajputana and Gujarat. He made Ajmer the headquarters for his operations in that region and enclosed it with strong ramparts and a moat.

Akbar was also a frequent visitor to the shrine of the great Muslim saint, Khwaja Mohinuddin Chisti. He once walked from Agra to this mausoleum, about two hundred miles, in fulfilment of a vow that he would undertake such a journey if a son was born to him. During his reign, a passage is supposed to have been constructed for the convenience of the royal harem. When the harem women walked along this from the palace to the *dargah* (or mausoleum), curtains were drawn to prevent shopkeepers and passers-by from gazing at them.

The Akbari Masjid and Phool Mahal (palace of flowers) were added to the *dargah* complex in Akbar's time. His son Jehangir also added some palaces to Ajmer and a mosque to the *dargah* grounds.

Ajmer is now an important place of pilgrimage for both Muslims and Hindus. The former come in large numbers for the Urs *mela* (fair) at the *dargah*, usually in May. And the Hindus come in October to Pushkar for the Kartik Purnima (autumn full moon) festival. Pushkar is about seven miles from Ajmer.

Khwaja Mohinuddin Chisti, born in the mid-twelfth century, was a native of Afghanistan, but brought up in Persia. When he was still a child, he lost his father. He distributed his little inheritance among the poor and became a fakir. In the course of his wanderings, he became a disciple of Khwaja Usman Chisti Harooni, whose mausoleum is at Mecca.

When he was in his fifties, Khwaja Mohinuddin returned to Afghanistan. From there he came to India with the army of Mohammed Ghori, when the latter invaded the country at the end of the twelfth century.

Chisti died in Ajmer in the thirteenth century, at the age of 97. His remains were interned in the cell in which he had lived, but no masonry tomb was built over it. Akbar, Jehangir and Shah Jehan, each in his reign, added mosques and embellishments to the *dargah* grounds. Shah Jehan erected the present splendid dome, and added the Jama Masjid in white marble. His favourite daughter, Jahanara, added the Begumi Dalan.

Every year the *dargah* is the scene of the Urs *mela*, when pilgrims congregate to commemorate the anniversary of the Khwaja's death. Great crowds come to seek the blessings of the divine.

At the *dargah*, the atmosphere of a Muslim religious congregation pervades. Offerings are received at practically every corner, *qawwalis* or religious choruses sung, and garlands of jasmine and roses are piled on to the tomb, which is covered with velvet and cloth of gold.

Quite different from this shrine, to which people also throng, is another mosque in Ajmer that has unique archaeological importance, quaintly named Adhai-Din-ka-Jhopra (two-and-a-half days' shed). It may have derived its name from the fact that fakirs from various places stayed there temporarily while visiting Ajmer, or because it was re-fashioned in two-and-a-half days for Mohammed Ghori to worship in. What makes it interesting is that it was originally a renowned seat of Sanskrit learning. The quadrangle that is now cloistered on all four sides once possessed a huge Brahminical temple. The original pillars and the roof of this pre-Muslim structure were permitted to remain but the rest of the original portions were demolished and much of the carvings on the remaining pillars defaced. A screen or façade was constructed at the entrance and this still remains.

Excavations in the grounds of this mosque have shown that it once contained well-built temples dating earlier than the eleventh century.

Come October and all roads from Ajmer lead to Pushkar, some seven miles away. Thousands of men, women and cattle assemble on the shores of Lake Pushkar. It is a sprawling, vital fiesta timed for the Kartik Purnima, the period of the autumn full moon. The Pushkar *mela* is at once an occasion for worship and trade, even match-making. Devotees come to bathe in the holy lake where Lord Brahma, the Hindu creator, is said to have performed a holy sacrifice, called the *yagna*. The lake is said to have appeared at the spot where a lotus fell from Brahma's hand.

Legend, and there is one for everything in Rajasthan, tells us how Kartik Purnima came to be celebrated. After the *yagna*, Pushkar became so holy that the greatest sinners could go to heaven by merely bathing and purifying themselves in it. Heaven, as expected, became rather crowded. The gods were peeved because men no longer cared for them or for their earthly duties since they could get to heaven without bothering about either. Brahma agreed that this state of affairs had to be amended. He then ordained that the period of salvation on earth would be from the eleventh day of the Kartik month in the Hindu calendar to the night of the full moon. Which is why the great fair is held at this time every year at Pushkar.

As the bathers have to spend five full days there, a good deal of trading is done on the side. Animals are bought and sold, camel cart races run, and shops set up. The government tourism department usually chips in with dances and pageants to add to the excitement of Pushkar. And at night, after having performed *puja* with them, devotees set hundreds of lighted oil lamps afloat on the waters of the lake.

The tradition is centuries old. Wrote the Emperor Jehangir in his *Tujuk-i-Jehangiri*, "While at Ajmer I visited nine times the mausoleum of the revered Khwaja, and fifteen times went to look at Pushkar lake . . . ."

Above: A pavement curio seller
in Jaipur.
Left: An overview of Jaipur.

Above: The Jantar Manter observatory, built by Jai Singh II in Jaipur.
Below: A snake charmer in the central lawns of the Rambagh Palace Hotel, Jaipur.

The gleaming spires of the City Palace complex viewed from the Hawa Mahal.

Above: Every afternoon *shehnai* players perform in one of the pavilions, a tradition that is now 200 years old.

Left: A brass door with panels depicting the Radha Krishna legend in the Chandra Mahal.

Facing page

Top: Another view of the Chandra Mahal allows a glimpse of arms arrayed to form the emblem of the old Jaipur state. Note the painted designs on the walls.

Below left: Colonel Bhowani Singh, son of the last Jaipur Maharaja, in ceremonial attire in the family's personal apartments in the City Palace.

Below right: A carved elephant at the entrance of the City Palace, Udaipur.

Above: The armoury at the Sileh Khana in the City Palace, Jaipur.
Below: The Hawa Mahal, or pavilion of winds, in the City Palace.

Above: A view of the fort at Amber, the old capital of the Kachhwaha dynasty.
Below: The Sheesh Mahal, or the Hall of Mirrors, in Amber.

Above: Jaigarh Fort crests the hill above Amber.

Left: The *dargah* of Mohinuddin Chisti at Ajmer.

Facing page

Top: A *qawwali* in progress at the *dargah*.

Below left: The Nahargarh Fort.

Below right: A *sadhu* meditating at the pool at Galta.

Page 84

A monkey perched on a temple window.

Bharatpur, Deeg, Alwar

RAJASTHAN VERY OFTEN ENSCONCES ITS LOVELIEST attractions in barren, rugged or dreary terrain. Bharatpur is, at first sight, an insignificant little town, with only the crumbling mud ramparts of a fortress to arouse interest. But people flock here every year, and viceroys, kings and princes came long before the tourists did.

A self-indulgent Maharaja, having savoured the duck-shooting spots of England, and deciding to have one of his own, gave Rajasthan a delightful sanctuary teeming with birds. In season, the birds are an eyeful, streaking across the sodden marsh, darting for fish and deafening the air with their cries.

The Keoladeo Ghana sanctuary, which gets its name from the Keoladeo temple of Lord Shiva, is eleven square miles of marsh and woodland. It was originally intended for duck-shooting, not bird-watching, by Maharaja Kishan Singh who came to power in Bharatpur state at the turn of the century. His guests shot them by the bagful. The place was declared a sanctuary in 1964.

There are a great many birds here, both exotic and common, and they are a delight to watch. Sarus cranes — gangling, red-capped and red-legged creatures — trumpet and prance in pairs in the rushes; snake-birds (darters) perch on short, thorny trees drying wet wings; and you might see a black-necked stork wading around clumsily, and coming up triumphantly with a wriggling fish in its long, black beak. The man who punts your boat through the marsh will tell you that it is the native birds who are non-vegetarian.

In season, which is roughly October to February, and particularly when they are breeding, one can get quite close to the birds because they do not fly away. Among them can be found the purple moorhen, the pheasant-tailed jacana, the flamingo, the brahminy duck, the painted stork and the egret. In October you see them nest-building, breeding in November-December, and a few weeks later teaching the young to fly. Winter visitors to the sanctuary include the elegant white Siberian crane, the greylag goose, also from Siberia, and the bar-headed goose, which breeds in western China and Central Asia in summer and comes down to India in winter.

To attract the birds to Bharatpur, Maharaja Kishan Singh had a dense forest flooded with water from the Gambir river during the rainy season, and then drained it out, leaving the lowlands filled with water. Muddy butts with shady trees were erected in these, intended for the use of hunters at the time of duck-shooting. Bushes of babool and other thorny trees were also planted in between. Some of these have begun to decay, and new saplings are now planted every year.

Shooting records engraved in stone can be found at the sanctuary. They tell you that a British peer, Lord Chemlsford, shot the largest number in a single shoot: 4,206 with 50 guns. The Prince of Wales, on his second shoot in 1921 did not do too badly either: 2,221 birds. Over the years, the Maharaja of Bharatpur's guests included royal visitors from Afghanistan, Iran, Malaysia and fellow maharajas from other states.

Bharatpur had other claims to fame before birds became its prime attraction. It was not a Rajput kingdom, but one carved out by the Jats. The early chroniclers record that the Jats, too, had a place in the ancient catalogue of 36 royal races, but the Rajputs consider them as primarily of sturdy peasant stock. A predominantly agricultural race, they are still the dominant community in Punjab Haryana and in parts of Rajasthan.

The history of the Jat rulers of Bharatpur is fairly recent compared to the rest of the Rajput provinces. Their dominion in this region originated in the Jat revolt against the bigotry of the Moghul Emperor Aurangzeb in the late seventeenth century. Two petty Jat chiefs trained their clansmen in group organization and open warfare. They built several small forts in the almost trackless jungles and strengthened these with mud walls that could defy artillery. The moat and mud walls of the fort at Bharatpur are an example of these.

In the turmoil that followed Aurangzeb's death, a Jat called Badan Singh carved Bharatpur out as a kingdom for himself. Its most illustrious ruler proved to be Suraj Mal, the son of a woman who was to become Badan Singh's favourite concubine. Enchanted by the mother, he adopted her infant, Suraj Mal, as his heir.

The forts at both Deeg and Bharatpur were built by Badan Singh, and it was Suraj Mal who laid the foundations of Bharatpur city and built the pleasure palaces at Deeg.

Badan Singh's fortress looks less imposing than the other magnificent specimens at Chittor, Jaisalmer or Kumbhalgarh. But it had some of the qualities of the man who built it — the sturdy simplicity and powerful strength of the Jats. In the early nineteenth century, it frustrated the celebrated British commander Lord Lake, who led a garrison to take Bharatpur. He did not succeed, though the siege lasted six weeks.

Today it can be entered by a drawbridge beneath which is a wide moat with some water still in it. The entrance gate with its fading murals of elephants, opens into a city within a city. One palace has been converted into a museum where archaeological finds from the five excavation sites around Bharatpur are displayed. Pottery and sculpture dating back to the second century BC have been discovered here. On the ground floor of the palace, adjoining the museum, is a brightly ornamented set of baths, or *hamams*, with panelled, painted walls and domes and separate sunken baths for hot and cold water. This is the only Rajput touch — for they loved using bright colours — in an otherwise austere Jat fortress.

The pleasure palaces of Deeg have been ranked by some as only second to the Taj Mahal in beauty and symmetry. There are stories about how these came to be built, none entirely plausible. One version is that it was built with the jewels and gold of the Nawab of Avadh (now Lucknow), entrusted by the Nawab to the Maharaja of Bharatpur for safe-keeping. The Nawab then went off on a pilgrimage to Mecca, and when he did not return for several years, Suraj Mal built the Deeg palaces with Avadh's wealth.

The pinkish brown palaces and pavilions with gold spires have been laid out among formal gardens, with a myriad of fountains. These are dry now, but with them working, Deeg must have been an idyllic refuge for the battle-weary kings of Bharatpur. An old retainer of the royal family of Bharatpur recalls that colourful chamois leather bags used to be placed at the base of these fountains to create sprays of many hues. Deeg was also the location for the Conrad Rooks film, "Siddartha", based on Herman Hesse's novel.

Architecturally, Deeg is considered unusual because of its double cornices. In one of the pavilions are square marble pillars inlaid with exquisite miniatures. These include portraits and figures. The *zenana* also has marble inlay. Gopal Bhavan, the main palace, overhangs a lake on one side. It is an unusual building with two storeys on the side facing the garden and four on the side facing the lake.

Symmetrical though it all seems, Deeg actually remains incomplete. As originally conceived, it was to be twice the area it is now, with a broad terrace linking two rectangles. What can be seen today is one rectangle, with water on both sides. Suraj Mal was slain in battle before he could add further to it.

From birds and palaces to tigers and ruins. Sariska and Alwar, some 75 miles from Deeg by road, are a natural corollary to a trip to Bharatpur and Deeg. For both Alwar and Bharatpur were once part of the region known as Mewat, the hilly, Jat-dominated north-eastern part of Rajputana. Alwar was once protected by ramparts and moats on all sides except on the hill side. The ramparts were levelled and the moats filled in around 1940. The town has a fort, but Alwar's best attractions are outside.

Sariska is a short drive from civilization into tiger country. A huge stretch of forested hills and valleys, approximately 110 square miles, went into the creation of this spreading sanctuary. And though the big cats are more elusive than the fidgety visitors atop the two watch-towers would want them to be, they do come down, particularly in the dry months, to the water-holes. Besides tigers, sambar, nilgai (blue bull), spotted deer and wild boar all roam the enclosure. A lovely relaxed weekend resort, the sanctuary also contains a twelfth century Shiva temple and an abandoned fort.

Archaeological evidence of this area having been part of the Mauryan empire in the third century BC exists at Bairath, a detour on the Alwar-Jaipur road. The remnants of a Buddhist monastery are found atop a plateau, the route to which is by a stone-paved path. At a lower level are the remains of a Buddhist chapel or *chaitya*, on a circular foundation. The great Mauryan Emperor Asoka was a convert to Buddhism and subsequently a tireless propagator of this religion. A minor rock edict of his time was found at Bairath.

This area also formed part of the dominion of the Indo-Bactrian Greeks. A small jar of coarse clay containing 36 ancient coins was discovered hidden in a wall during excavations at Bairath. Twenty-eight of these were found to be of Greek and Indo-Greek kings. For good measure, Bairath also figures in the ancient Indian epic, the *Mahabharata*.

A snake bird dries its wings after a catch in the Bharatpur sanctuary.

Facing page
Top left: A bird on the wing.
Top right: Stone carvings in the palace museum within Bharatpur fort.
Bottom: Murals at the entrance to Bharatpur Fort.

Above: More stone carvings in the palace museum.
Right: Marble pillars with inlaid miniatures in the Nand and Bhavan Deeg palaces.

Above: The Suraj Bhavan.
Left: The Bhadon Pavilion, with the Gopal Sagar tank in the background.
Opposite: The Lakshman temple in Deeg.

The Hoodanga festival, celebrated a week after Holi at Deeg.

Jaisalmer, Jodhpur, Bikaner

"OUR WATER WAS CARRIED IN LEATHERN BAGS made of the skins of sheep, besides some much larger ones, made of the hides of oxen, and twenty-four large copper vessels, two of which were a load for a camel. Our marches were seldom very long. The longest was twenty-six miles, and shortest fifteen, but the fatigue which our people bore suffered no proportion to the distance. Our line, when in closest order, was two miles long. The path by which we travelled, wound much to avoid the sandhills. It was too narrow to allow of two camels going abreast; and if an animal stepped to one side, it sank in the sand as in snow."

Not much has changed in the heart of the Thar since Mounstuart Elphinstone, a British civil servant, wrote this account of his traverse through the Indian desert in 1809. Water is still a scarce and precious commodity: wells are hundreds of feet deep, and it rains so infrequently that local people tell you many children here have never seen a rain shower. The camel is still the common man's vehicle, and people in villages near Jaisalmer are even today wary of parts of the desert where camels have been known to sink completely into the sand.

Desert Rajasthan is stark and grim, but it is also spectacular. It has three cities spaced out over a thousand square miles of sand and scrub—one terra-cotta pink, another pinkish brown, and the third a dull gold. Each of these is well worth the heat and dust, and none is a substitute for the other.

This is Marwar as distinct from Mewar, a land dominated around Jodhpur and Bikaner by the Rathor clan, and further west at Jaisalmer by another clan called the Bhattis. The name Marwar is thought to be derived from Maru—desert.

The oldest of the three towns is Jaisalmer. It is stark, small and stunning. Every single wall, building, and stone here is the colour of the desert sand. Less than three square miles in area, it has few people, a good many camels, and a massive, memorable fortress that dominates the landscape. Within the town's narrow, almost deserted lanes are the buildings that led one writer to describe Jaisalmer as a "filigreed stone gem-set in the desert."

Once the homes of wealthy merchants, these *havelis* have lace-like façades of the same yellow stone, fretted into an endless combination of geometrical patterns. Salim Singh ki Haveli is three storeys high, each canopied balcony minutely carved down to the last bracket. It is the incongruously beautiful legacy of a rapacious merchant.

This part of Rajputana, barren though it was, derived considerable wealth from being on the main camel caravan routes from Africa, Egypt, Arabia, Iran and Afghanistan to Delhi and Agra. Jaisalmer's rulers levied taxes upon these caravans, and here merchants thrived on trade and usury.

The Rajput clan that ruled in this part of the desert were the Bhattis. The only explanation on record of how they came to be there is rooted in mythology. The Bhattis claim descent from the lunar race called the Yadavs in the epic, *Mahabharata*. The head of this race was supposed to be Lord Krishna. When Krishna's holy city Dwaraka was reclaimed by the sea, the Yadavs are supposed to have scattered and migrated westwards to West Asia. Centuries later their descendants, the Bhattis, were supposed to have gradually migrated eastwards back into India.

The Bhatti rulers were called Rawals, even as those of Mewar were called Ranas. Jaisal, the founder of the city, was a Bhatti prince who usurped power from his nephew in the mid-twelfth century. Shortly after, he decided to shift his capital from Lodurva, the original capital of the Bhattis, because it was susceptible to invasions.

Rajasthan has no dearth of legends which give the Rajputs a divine dimension, and there is one such tale concerning the choice of the triple-peaked hill called Tricuta for the site of Jaisal's new capital. This is the mound on which the fortress was later built.

While seeking a site better adapted for defence than Lodurva, Jaisal came upon a hermit who told him the story of the triple-peaked hill that overlooked his hermitage. The Lord Krishna had once come there for a great sacrifice, and prophesied that in some distant age, a descendant of his clan would erect a castle on that mount and found a town there. On the same occasion, Krishna had smitten a rock with his discus, and sweet spring water had gushed forth.

The hermit now took Jaisal to this stream and showed him engraved on a rock, the following prophetic stanzas: "O Prince of Yadu vansa (dynasty) come into this land, and on this mountain top erect a triangular castle. Prince, whose name is Jaisal, who will be of Yadu race, abandon Lodorpura, here erect thy dwelling" (Tod's translation).

Jaisal obviously did not need any more persuading. He abandoned Lodurva and laid the foundation of the present fortress on this mount. Today, this fortress is a self-contained township, with people living within it, in houses built by their ancestors. It has palaces and several Jain and Hindu temples. The former are profusely ornamented, as always, and are also veritable treasure houses of ancient palm leaf manuscripts and treatises which are kept locked in their vaults.

The massive walls of the fort are supposed to have been built of stone blocks merely arranged on top of each other, without any cementing material. The huge stone balls that one sees at regular intervals along the boundary wall were ammunition, in a sense. In the event of an attack, these were pushed down onto advancing soldiers. Following a delightful children's film shot here on location by the noted Indian director Satyajit Ray, the Jaisalmer fort is now popularly called "Sonar Kella" (Golden Fortress), from the title of the film.

Lodurva, the old capital, is about an hour's drive from Jaisalmer. It is largely in ruins, and the river that once flowed through here has dried up. But it has a beautiful Jain temple which draws a large number of pilgrims. What makes this temple unique, more so than the ones in Jaisalmer fort, is its star-shaped ground plan, and walls of the circumambulatory which incline outwards from the base. It also has windows in the roof which allow light to filter into the innermost sanctum, which is usually supposed to be dark.

Closer to Jaisalmer than Lodurva is a reservoir built by a six-teenth century Maharawal called Amar Singh. There are the remains of a building above the wall of the reservoir, which has animal heads sculpted on it at intervals. These acted as markers for the water level. This complex includes a Jain temple, cenotaphs, and several *baolis* or very old wells.

The nearest patch of classic, rippled sand dunes is at Sam, about twenty-seven miles from Jaisalmer. Rajasthan's Department of Tourism organizes a desert festival in February, which features camel rides over the dunes at Sam, as well as a pageant and a barbecue. And finally, there is a wood fossil park not far from Jaisalmer, near a village called Akal, where wood fossils in various stages of formation have been found.

On the way to Jodhpur from Jaisalmer, is Pokharan. There is a fort here, but Pokharan is best known today as the site of India's only underground atomic explosion.

Jodhpur's lofty fort looms in the distance long before one enters the city. From the top of this fort, contemporary historians say, Rao Jodha, the city's founder, and his sons after him, could see up to the limits of their sway. The height of this scarped summit is considerable — before it became the site of the citadel this projection was known as Bakharchiriya, or the bird's nest.

Jodhpur was the citadel of the Rathores (see chapter on History) and their rapid expansion across and consolidation over Marwar is a good example of the benefits of numerous progeny. Two Rathors rode out from Gujarat in the thirteenth century, with two hundred retainers, partly as a pilgrimage, partly to seek their fortunes elsewhere. Their adventures in Marwar, then ruled by another clan, led to one of them, Siahji, marrying and expanding his lineage in this region. He had three sons, and eight grandsons, each of whom in turn multiplied fruitfully.

A century later there were enough Rathors around for a descendant of Siahji, Chonda, to round them up and muster a substantial force. With their help he was able to establish Rathor supremacy in the capital, then Mandore. He married a princess of the ruling clan, had fourteen sons, and firmly established the line of Rathors in Marwar.

Jodha, who was to found Jodhpur, was Chonda's grandson. He shifted the capital from Mandore to Jodhpur for the same reason that Jaisal shifted his from Lodurva — the older capital was not sufficiently immune to invasion. And again, the suggestion for the location of a new capital came from a hermit.

The fortress is tremendously impressive, rising above a terrifyingly sheer base. The palaces inside are as beautifully ornate as the exterior is rugged, and the *jali* or fretwork that adorns the *havelis* of Jaisalmer is to be seen here again. The two palaces, with evocative names — the Pearl Palace and the Flower Palace — have designs painted on the walls and ceilings.

Jodhpur is less striking than Jaisalmer, but more pleasant. The city has a number of graceful, pinkish-brown buildings that now house the machinery of government.

Mandore, the old capital, is located on the same range as the new one, but on a less steep elevation. The way up to its ruins is through a gently sloping, shady, partly wild, garden. Here one finds a shrine which offers a pictorial exhibition of Rajasthan's mythology within two galleries called the Hall of Heroes, and the Hall of Gods. All those deities, heroes and saints who figure in Rajasthan's folklore have been immortalised here, in bright, gaudy, life-sized images.

At the entrance to the Mandore gardens are the cenotaphs of the Raos of Jodhpur. These are chronologically arranged so that they ascend steadily in height with each successive Rao, until the peak is reached with the cenotaph of Rao Ajit Singh, who fought successfully against the Moghul Emperor Aurangzeb's troops.

About forty miles from Jodhpur is an important group of Brahminical Jain temples called Osian, the earliest of which date back to the eighth century (see chapter on Architecture).

Bikaner lies north of Jodhpur, its reddish-pink stone rising out of miles of barren thorn and scrub. Rao Jodha's sixth son, Bika, must have found nothing more than this wilderness when he rode out here in search of pastures to conquer, but he was obviously undeterred.

He set out from Mandore the same year that his father shifted his capital to Jodhpur. Bika took with him three hundred zealous retainers, and they massacred the first opposing clan they encountered. Then they came into contact with a branch of the Bhattis of Jaisalmer, who had settled in this region, and Bika married a daughter of the chief. Using their settlement as a base, he was able to gradually augment his conquests in this region.

He encountered the Jats, a sturdy peasant race who had settled in this region ages ago. Bika's conquest of them is recorded to have been a bloodless one. Rivalry among the Jat communities led some of them to negotiate with the Rathor, accepting supremacy in return for protection. Having secured their submission, and those of the Bhattis in the region, he founded his capital, Bikaner, here.

In a sense, Bikaner is as much a pink city as Jaipur, though the colour is a few shades deeper here, and a lot more pervasive. It has everything that the other desert cities have to offer — a fortress, palaces and cenotaphs. It also has a museum and an archive with exceptionally good collections.

But the best attraction is the huge camel breeding farm. This is a government venture to supply quality animals to the local populace. The camels are taken out to graze all day and canter home at sunset, single file, heading for the feeding trough. The air comes alive with their grunts. The baby camels feed with their mothers at a separate trough. Visitors are offered a fresh glass of camel milk. The animals reared here fetch a handsome price.

Bikaner's other unique attraction is a temple calculated to make one shudder. Twelve miles away, at a place called Deshnoke, is a temple of the family deity of the Bikaner rulers. Karni Devi was a mystic *charan* or bard. She had performed several miracles in her lifetime but there was one occasion when she failed. She could not bring a dead boy back to life, because the God of Death, Yama, would not yield to her the soul of the boy, who he said had already been reincarnated. Incensed, Karni Devi vowed that none of her tribe (*charans*) would ever come under the jurisdiction of the God of Death again. Instead, when they died, their souls would inhabit the bodies of rats. That was the origin of the tradition of holding rats sacred in this temple. The shrine is awash with hundreds of scurrying rats who are fed and held sacred, for they are thought to house the souls of bards. The rulers of Bikaner have lavished attention on this shrine: it has a carved marble façade, gates made of silver and a canopy for the deity made of gold.

Bikaner's fort is in the heart of the city. It was built by a ruler called Rai Singh who was a general at the court of the Moghul Emperor Akbar. It has a long range of pavilions which appear above the sturdy outer wall, and palaces that are beautifully embellished with paintings, mirror-work, and lacquer-work.

The nineteenth century Lalgarh, more a palace than a fort, was the home of Bikaner's most illustrious ruler in recent times, Maharaja Ganga Singh. He built the Ganganagar Canal, a pioneering effort to ensure this desert city year-round water supply. But a far more gigantic effort is now in progress in this region. With the aid of the World Bank, the Rajasthan Canal will link Punjab to Rajasthan and make hundreds of arid acres irrigable. It is one of the biggest ventures of its kind in the world. Its nearest point to Bikaner is a few hours' drive from the city.

Left: A Bhil couple in a Jaisalmer street.
Right: Lime paste adorns the doorway of a house.

Left: Jaisalmer's famed "golden fortress" built from the local yellow sandstone.
Below: The city seen from the ramparts of the fort.

Facing page
Top: The Putwon ki Haveli in Jaisalmer.
Bottom left: Inside a house in Jaisalmer Fort.

Right: Turquoise embellishments on a house within Jaisalmer Fort.
Below: Marble throne within the fort used by the Bhatti dynasty rulers when holding public audiences.

Facing page
An old man leads his camel past the *havelis* in Jaisalmer.

Above left: The Umaid Vilas in Jodhpur
Fort.
Above right: The throne in the Moti
Mahal in Jodhpur Fort. In the background
is a stained-glass door.
Left: The Phool Mahal in Jodhpur Fort.

Facing face
Top: The Sardar Vilas in Jodhpur Fort.
Bottom: A street procession in Jodhpur.

Above left: The Shrine of a Million Gods at Mandore.
Above right: A Bikaner street at night.
Left: The rat temple dedicated to the goddess Karni Devi at Deshnoke near Bikaner.

Udaipur and Chittorgarh

IF THERE WAS ONE RAJPUT KING WHO FAILED TO live up to the legendary courage and heroism of the Rajputs, it was Rana Udai Singh. When Akbar's troops fell upon Chittor, Udai Singh fled.

Little wonder then that the city built by this man in a vale of the Aravallis should have none of the rugged masculinity of Rajputana's citadel towns. Far from being a drawback, this is precisely Udaipur's charm. It is a serene, graceful city whose slender-pillared and domed palaces are mirrored in a girdle of placid artificial lakes. Ramparts and battlements do not dominate, water and greenery do.

Chittor has what Udaipur misses. It is as ruggedly attractive as the latter is quietly beautiful. Both have at different times been capitals of Mewar and have given rise to some of Rajasthan's best-loved legends. Taken together with Kumbhalgarh, Rana Kumbha's famous, once invincible cliff-top fortress, this part of Rajasthan could give anyone a memorable holiday.

A splendid fortress rises steeply from the surrounding countryside, and runs along the crest of this elevation for three miles or more. A lot of blood has been spilt here, for Chittor was sacked three times by Muslim invaders while it remained the capital of Mewar. It was also Chittor that gave Mewar and the country one of the most illustrious rulers ever, Maharana Kumbha.

Kumbha, whose full name was Kumbhakarna, ruled for thirty-five years in the mid-fifteenth century and belonged to the Guhilot or Sisodia clan, which is one of the solar races of the Rajputs. His best claim to posterity was his patronage of architecture — Fort Kumbhalgarh in southern Udaipur district, Fort Achalgarh in Abu, the unique Jain temple at Ranakpur, the Tower of Victory or Fame at Chittor, and the improvements to the fort at Chittor were all done during his reign.

But he was also a considerable warrior, a scholar who has written several treatises, and an accomplished musician.

Chittorgarh is the earliest fort on record in Rajasthan, and is traditionally ascribed a mythological origin. Kumbha strengthened its defences and built some of its gates. He added a proper road, and wells and reservoirs that gave it an abundant supply of water.

Also at Chittor are two sculptured towers; one was erected by Kumbha to commemorate his victory in battle over Sultan Mahmud Khilji of Malwa (now outside Rajasthan) and the other, a Jain tower built much earlier. Kumbha's tower, known both as Jayasthambha (tower of victory) and Kirtistambha (tower of fame) has nine storeys and took six years to build. Each storey has doors with colonnaded porticos, trellis windows and statues and ornaments. It is built mainly of compact limestone and the quartz rock on which it stands. The ninth storey has a vault with a sculptured representation of the Lord Krishna surrounded by dancing *gopies*, or muses. The entire tower is profusely decorated with carvings.

The Jain tower at Chittor was probably built in the twelfth century. It has four storeys, and is dedicated to the first Jain saint, Adinath. Nude figures of him are repeated hundreds of times all over the tower.

Inside the fortress there is also a temple associated with Mirabai, a mystic who, by one account, was the wife of Rana Kumbha, and by another, the wife of his grandson Bhoja. Her hymns, composed in ecstatic devotion to Lord Krishna, are still sung by devotees.

The palace of Padmini at Chittor evokes the single most famous legend concerning this city. Padmini, the wife of Bhim Singh, a thirteenth-century regent of a minor king, was a fabled beauty, and the conqueror Allaudin Khilji was obsessed with the desire to possess her. There is some difference of opinion as to whether Padmini or the desire for territorial expansion was the reason for Allaudin's siege of Chittor, or both. At any rate, after a long and fruitless siege, he agreed to be content with merely a glimpse of her. The Rajputs' strict rule about *purdah* for married women could not permit an infidel to gaze directly upon one of their women, so a glimpse of her reflection in a mirror was permitted.

That over, Bhim Singh courteously escorted his enemy to the foot of the fortress, an instance of the sort of misguided chivalry the

Rajputs loved to indulge in. Once outside, he was ambushed and captured. Allaudin demanded Padmini as ransom. She acquiesced, and a procession of palanquins ostensibly bearing her and her hand-maidens wound its way into Allaudin's camp. When the palanquins were lowered, however, there alighted from them not maidens but armed soldiers. In the confusion that followed, Bhim Singh escaped.

. Allaudin did not take kindly to being tricked in this fashion. He stormed the fort with vengeance. Padmini gathered all the women in the stronghold together and they committed *jauhar*, a rite of immolation to forestall disgrace, in a subterranean cave.

Chittor was sacked again in the early sixteenth century by the Sultan of Gujarat, and again thousands of women perished in the *jauhar* led by the mother of the infant Udai Singh who was to later found Udaipur. Udai Singh escaped due to his faithful nurse, Panna, who while the palace was being stormed, substituted her own child in Udai Singh's cradle and had the heir to Chittor smuggled out of the palace grounds in a basket covered with leaves. Her own child was killed.

After wandering from chieftain to chieftain to seek protection for her charge, she ended up at Kumbhalgarh, where the governor accepted the lad and brought him up as his nephew. Around the middle of the sixteenth century, Udai Singh was recognized as the true heir and reinstated at Chittor.

Thirty years later, the Emperor Akbar struck the final, fatal blow to the rugged citadel that had been the pride of Mewar. Udai Singh earned himself the reputation of a coward when he deserted, leaving the defence of the city to two youthful chieftains. These two, Jaimall and Patta, both barely sixteen years of age, displayed desperate valour and died fighting. They were not alone. As if not to be outdone, Patta's mother and bride also entered the fray and perished.

Chittor saw so much defiant bravery and death in three decades of its history that one is likely to get the impression that the Rajputs often indulged in martial valour for its own sake, heedless of the consequences. The terrible *jauhars* in which women perished were accompanied by the remaining men donning saffron robes and throwing open the gates of the fort to the enemy, so that they could all die fighting.

Udai Singh, of course, seems to have been something of an

exception to this general rule. His claim to posterity is that he founded Udaipur in a valley of the Aravallis. This city is at its most beautiful from September onwards, at the tail-end of the monsoons. It is ringed all around with hills, and the lakes around which the city sprang up are full during this season. Rana Udai Singh's choice of the site was mainly guided by the existence of this girdle of hills and a lake. The rest of the four lakes were later artificial creations.

The city palace of Udaipur was originally founded by Rana Udai Singh in the form of a small citadel. It gradually expanded into a massive edifice overlooking Pichola lake. It has fluted turrets and balconies supported on carved brackets projecting from the mass of masonry that faces the lake. Inside, it is quite magnificent, with a garden complete with trees and a pond on one of the higher storeys —possible because the citadel is built around the hillock, and the garden is the crest of this hillock.

The palace is rich in individual attractions, such as the Krishna Vilas, a small room whose entire wall surface is covered with painted miniatures of festivals, processions and scenes of royal pastimes. It was done in memory of a young princess who became a pawn in the ambitious games of two rival, neighbouring clans. Her name was Krishna Kumari, and her father was one of Mewar's later rulers, in the early nineteenth century. By then, the state had been considerably weakened politically, and beset by enemies. Two rival powers, those of Jaipur and Jodhpur, demanded the sixteen-year-old Krishna Kumari's hand in marriage. To favour either would have meant asking for war. The young girl herself provided the way out—she resolved to poison herself. As Tod tells it, the draught had to be prepared three times because the poison failed to take effect. Finally, she called for the opiate extract of poppy blossoms and died. Her heartbroken mother died soon after, and her father had her room frescoed in her memory.

The other display of exquisite workmanship is found in the Mor Chowk or peacock square, where mosaic and enamel combine in a brilliant display of peacocks depicting the three seasons.

The palace also has what it calls a Chini Chitrashala or Chinese picture gallery, with panels of delicate Chinese blue and white tiles. Looking out onto the lake, one can see the Jag Nivas Lake Palace, now a unique hotel which can be approached only by boat. The writer Pearl Buck is said to have once rented the best suite here to work on a novel.

Saheliyon ki Bari, or the garden of the maids of honour, was created for a princess who loved rain, or so one story goes. It has myriads of invisible fountains along pathways, around paved circles where the princess could sit, and next to foliage. Close your eyes when the fountains are turned on, and you can hear the patter of rain on leaves. The water comes from one of the city's lakes some distance away, through pipes that have survived the years, and is forced through the fountain jets because the lake is at a higher altitude than the garden.

The cenotaphs of the rulers of Mewar are just outside Udaipur at Ahar (see chapter on Architecture).

The two most important religious places in Mewar, Eklinji and Nathdwara, are both excursions north of Udaipur. The temple of Eklinji, who was the deity of the Ranas of Mewar and an incarnation of Shiva, is about thirteen miles from Udaipur. The founder of the Sisodia clan in Mewar, Bappa Rawal, is credited with having built the original temple, which has since been rebuilt and refurbished by successive maharanas, including Kumbha.

The design of the temple is considered somewhat unusual, with a double-storeyed sanctuary. The porch is covered by a pyramidical roof of many hundred circular knobs. The main shrine is of white marble, the deity of black.

Nathdwara, literally 'portal of the god', is thirty miles north of Udaipur, an important place of pilgrimage and a town where a number of beautiful crafts flourish. In the latter half of the seventeenth century, in anticipation of a raid by the Moghul Emperor Aurangzeb on Mathura, an ancient image of the Lord Krishna was removed by the then Rana of Mewar. The Rana wanted the image out of danger's way and it was sent on a cart to Mewar. The cart got stuck when it reached a village called Siarh, and this was interpreted to mean that the God wanted to remain there. The famous temple came to be built here, and the place was renamed Nathdwara.

The sacred image in the temple is sculpted from one piece of black marble. The vestments and ornaments of this deity are changed several times a day for the various *pujas* held here. This is a very wealthy temple and its head priest holds a paramount position among the followers of Vaishnavism, the cult of Vishnu the preserver.

Folk paintings of the deity, done in various mediums, constitute a flourishing cottage industry in this temple-town. Much of the delicate Rajasthani *meenakari*, or enamelled jewellery, sold in Udaipur and Jaipur is also fashioned by craftsmen here.

North-east of Udaipur is that marvellous, rough-hewn fortress called Kumbhalgarh. It is difficult to get to this fort, and therefore easy to understand why the Maharanas of Mewar always turned to it when Udaipur became unsafe and Chittor untenable. Situated on a high peak of the most westerly range of the Aravalli hills, it is hemmed in by other ranges and impressively fortified. Access to the fortress can be made by jeep.

The defences consist of a series of walls with battlements and bastions built on the slopes of a hill. The bastions were so designed that the enemy would not be able to scale them with ladders, and the high battlement walks were so thick that eight horsemen could ride abreast on them.

Kumbhalgarh contains a domed palace and buildings which are reached through several gateways along a winding approach. The topmost palace is in surprising contrast to the general ruggedness of the surroundings. It has beautiful suites of rooms rebuilt by a successor in the late nineteenth century in lovely pastel shades. Within the grounds of the fortress are the ruins of Jain temples, reservoirs and barracks for the garrison.

Kumbhalgarh is considered the best example of Rana Kumbha's military genius. His successors sent their royal households to this fortress when the might of the Moghul empire was pitted against them. It fell only once, to the combined might of Akbar and the Rajput princes of Marwar and Amber, who had aligned themselves with the Moghul against Rana Pratap.

Pratap, the son of Udai Singh, is a much loved hero in Mewar. For, while his father had fled Chittor and established a new capital, Pratap was obsessed by the desire to win back the old capital, and pitted himself against Akbar, who was the mightiest Moghul emperor of them all.

Akbar's siege against Pratap at Kumbhalgarh succeeded more on the basis of treachery than military might. According to one account, the aggressors succeeded in contaminating the sole water resource of the fortress by introducing insects. The travails of Rana Pratap and his steadfast refusal to make peace with the Moghuls, even though it cost him years of uncomfortable exile, are part of the folklore of Mewar. The battle of Haldighati, in which he took on the Moghul forces, is still celebrated in murals and paintings in the City Palace of Udaipur. It was a grim battle in which most of Pratap's forces were killed, while he escaped death only by fleeing on his gallant steed, Chetak. The horse is supposed to have leapt across a mountain stream with his master when closely pursued by two Moghul chiefs. Chetak was wounded and died after this effort, but not before he had seen his master out of danger. A memorial has since been built on the spot where Chetak died. An even more contemporary tribute is the daily train from Delhi to Udaipur, which is named after this horse.

A grim period in exile followed Pratap's defeat at Haldighati and the siege of Kumbhalgarh, during which he escaped from the fortress by a secret passage. He spent years hiding out in the hills with his family, often with the help of the Bhil tribes who once hid his children in wicker baskets suspended from trees to save them from tigers and wolves.

Finally, Pratap was able to regain Kumbhalgarh and Udaipur, but not Chittor. Udaipur has more memorials to Rana Pratap, who was cast in the mould of a true Rajput valiant, than to its founder. The City Palace has his armour and a galaxy of pictures recreating the battle of Haldighati. And higher than the rest of the city is Chetak Circle, where a horse rears with his master on his back, in a garden full of flowers. At Chavand, a village some sixty miles south of Udaipur, is another memorial to the warrior and his horse. Chavand is where Pratap sought refuge during his exile. The battlefield of Haldighati, too, now survives as a memorial.

The *Jai Stambh*, or victory tower, at Chittor.

Above: Udaipur city with the palace in the background.
Below: A mural on the gateway of the City Palace, Udaipur.

Details in the City Palace:
Left: Idol of Ganesh Deodi in the City Palace.
Below: A hand-pulled *punkah* (fan).
Right: The Manak Mahal.
Below right: The Mor Chowk.

Left: The painted wall of Krishna Vilas in the Udaipur Palace.

Below: Chinese tiles decorate the Chini Chitrashala balcony in the City Palace.

Facing page

Top: A view of the Maharani suite of the Lake Palace Hotel, Udaipur.

Bottom left: A priest distributes *prasad* outside the famous temple of Lord Krishna at Nathdwara.

Bottom right: Women sleeping outside a Ganesh temple at Nathdwara.

Abu and Ranakpur

Tod CALLS ABU, WITH ITS CLUSTER OF FAMOUS temples, the "Olympus of the Hindus". The Aravalli hills stretching from Delhi to Gujarat reach their highest point here in a mountain, atop which is a picturesque plateau. This is Abu, a lovely lush green summer resort and the only hill station in Rajasthan. Mount Abu has a somewhat steep ascent, with ravines cut into its sides, which are filled with tree bushes and beautiful birds. It is a detached hill, and the plateau atop the summit is cut with granite rocks of fantastic shapes, the space between them greened over.

As a place of pilgrimage for the Jain community, which built a cluster of temples here, Abu has always been the most important place in the kingdom of Sirohi. The rulers of Sirohi belonged to a branch of the Chauhan Rajputs.

Legend has it that Abu is where the four Agnikula, or fire-born, clans had their origin. Brahmin priests created these Rajput warrior clans out of a fire-pit to rid the earth of demons, or so the story goes. The Chauhans, Pramaras, Pratiharas and Solankis are said to be the clans so created. The spot hallowed by this legend is Gaumukh, some distance on foot from the temple of Hanuman, the monkey god.

Abu was susceptible to conquest despite its isolated elevation, and passed through the hands of several dynasties before it came into the possession of Chauhan rulers. A descendant of this line clashed with Maharana Kumbha of Mewar, who eventually conquered Abu and, according to an inscription on the Tower of Victory at Chittor, built the fort of Achalgarh on the summit of a hill.

Mount Abu's chief claim to fame, however, are the Jain temples at Dilwara, about two miles from the lovely, artificial Nakki lake, which too has a legend behind its name. Nakki means 'nails', and the lake is supposed to have been dug by the gods with their nails.

The Dilwara temples were built during the age of Jain supremacy. Two of these have been singled out by historians and students of architecture as particularly outstanding. These are the temple of Vimala, dedicated to the first Jain *tirthankar*, Adinath, and another temple built later, dedicated to the twenty-second *tirthankar*, Neminath.

Vimala has been variously described as a wealthy merchant and as a minister of state in the eleventh century. While the temple is not particularly remarkable on the outside, the inside more than makes up for the exterior plainness. One enters the temple through a domed porch on the east, and comes out onto a six-pillared pavilion with a three-tiered *samosan*, or a conventional representation of the holy mountain of the Jains, in the centre, surrounded by ten statues of the founder, Vimala, and his family. Each of these is seated on an elephant, chiselled out of single blocks of white marble, about four feet high. On each elephant the figure is seated in an elaborately carved howda behind the mahout. These representations are now badly defaced, having been destroyed by Muslim zealots.

This temple is supposed to be one of the oldest and most complete example of a Jain temple. From the pavilion, one passes into a cloistered courtyard. Here the temple resolves itself into a grouping of pillars which form an open portico and vestibule beyond which is an enclosed portion containing the shrine.

This is lit only from the door, and contains a cross-legged, seated figure of Jina Adinath, to whom the temple is dedicated. Practically every surface of the interior of this temple, including the pillars, is very elaborately carved. But what sets it apart is the splendour of the domed ceiling of the hall. Percy Brown, in his *Indian Architecture (Buddhist and Hindu Period)* details the profusion of imagery that went into this ornate ceiling.

"This dome is built up of eleven concentric rings, five of which, interposed at regular intervals, depict patterns of figures and animals . . . . The lowest contains the forefronts of elephants, their trunks intertwined, as many as a hundred and fifty of these in close ranks. A few mouldings above is another border representing images in niches, also repeated many times, and again over that, a similar course of dancing figures. This is followed higher up in the concavity by a series of horsemen, finishing in the topmost storey with more figures engaged in an endless dance. Between these various figured courses are ornamental repeats, gradually becoming more pronounced until towards the apex they culminate in a grouping of pendants not unlike festoons of foliage suspended from the high trees of a forest."

So much for the minute details. Superimposed upon all this, athwart the outer concentric rings, are sixteen brackets that easily catch the eye. Each of these is a female figure, representing a Vidyadevi, or goddess of knowledge.

The later Neminath temple, also in the Dilwara group, is said to have been built by two brothers, Tejpala and Vasupala, whose names are also associated with the famous triple temple at Girnar in Gujarat. The inscriptions in this temple, however, ascribe its erection and endowment to Tejpala, in memory of his brother. The inscription records that it was consecrated in AD 1230.

A visitor bent on taking in the best of Rajasthan's temple wealth has also to go to Ranakpur, about a hundred miles from Udaipur, but also negotiable from Abu, via Sirohi. In locating their shrines, the Jains chose both summits and glens. Some of their favourite *tirthas* are found in deep, secluded valleys, and those in Ranakpur belong to this category.

Maharana Kumbha, the illustrious ruler of Mewar who gave Rajasthan both the Kumbhalgarh fort and the Tower of Victory at Chittor, among other beautiful buildings, was also a liberal patron of the Jain community. It was in his reign that the most important temple at Ranakpur was built. The Chaumukha temple, like the Vimala temple at Abu, is dedicated to the first Jain *tirthankar*, Adinath. Chaumukha literally means 'four-faced'. It is considered the most complex and extensive Jain temple in India.

Apart from the architectural features, the Chaumukha temple has several inscriptions which make it an important historical source. One of these in Sanskrit, close to the entrance of the main shrine on the right, gives details of the temple's origin.

It was supposed to have been built by a devout Jain called Dharmaka, who one night dreamt of a celestial car. Wanting to capture the image he had dreamt, he called several architects, gave them a description and asked them to reproduce it. Of the plans that were subsequently produced, all were rejected except that of a Brahmin called Dipaka. What this man had reconstructed was apparently exactly like the celestial car Dharmaka had seen in his dream. It was originally intended to have seven storeys, but only four were completed, including the subterranean vault.

The Chaumukha temple is a massive creation. It covers over forty thousand square feet, and has twenty-nine halls containing four hundred and twenty pillars. The designs on no two of these are exactly alike. It is built on a very high plinth, with a lofty boundary wall which recalls the battlemented fortifications of temple cities. There are, however, graceful turrets rising from this wall, and each of these corresponds to a cell on the inner face of the wall.

Seen from outside, five *shikaras*, or spires, rise above the walls, and some twenty cupolas, each forming the roof of a pillared hall. Each *shikara*, of course, represents a shrine below, with the largest and most prominent surmounting the central sanctuary.

The temple has three entrances with double-storeyed portals. Each of these leads through a series of columned courts into the main halls of the temple proper. When you get to the heart of the whole labyrinth, the confusion of pillars and halls sorts itself out. It becomes clear that there is a central sanctuary surrounded by a range of chapels and subsidiary shrines. Inside the main temple, in a hall with a hundred pillars is the chamber where the Chaumukha is enshrined. There are four entrances, and the Chaumukha itself is a quadrupled image, in white marble, of Adinath.

The temple is built mainly in two storeys with portions of it rising to a third storey. The rectangular courtyard surrounding the main temple is open to the sky. With its myriad pillars and broad caves, the interior of the temple presents a fascinating interplay of light and shade. As might be expected, every portion of the temple is profusely and intricately carved.

There is also a sun temple at Ranakpur, some distance from the Jain shrines. Its sanctum and hall are polygonal, embellished with a running band of solar deities seated in racing chariots.

Above: The ceiling of the temple of
Vimala in Abu.
Left: Detail from a pillar in the temple
of Vimala.

Facing page
Top: Spires of the Chaumukha Jain temple
at Ranakpur.
Bottom: Detail of the exquisitely carved
ceiling of the main sanctuary of the
Chaumukha Jain temple.

The Head Priest at the Chaumukha temple.